The Diary of Edwin Clarke

A police officer in Rhodesia, 1906

Edwin Gulliver Clarke

The Diary of Edwin Clarke

A police officer in Rhodesia, 1906

JEPPESTOWN

INTRODUCTION

At the time he began this diary, Edwin Gulliver Clarke was 22, and had three years' service as a trooper in the British South Africa Police BSAP). Clarke came from an middle-class English background: the son of a bank manager from Aylesbury, he joined the 21st Lancers in 1900 during the Boer War, and was discharged as medically unfit less than a year later, most likely in Cape Town. He applied to join the BSAP, and attested as a trooper for an initial three-year period in November 1901, aged 18, with the regimental number 245. He signed on for another two years in 1904, when he was serving in Gwanda, and another two-and-a-half years in November 1906, in Bulawayo. However, Clarke bought himself out just seven months later, leaving the service in June 1907.

After Rhodesia it seems that Clarke emigrated to Canada in around 1910, living in Calgary, where he married, and soldiered part-time in the 19th Alberta Dragoons militia regiment; at some point he was joined in Canada by one of his younger brothers, Arthur. On the outbreak of the First World War in 1914, both brothers joined Princess Patricia's Canadian Light Infantry, and embarked for Europe in October 1914 with the Canadian Expeditionary Force. Edwin Clarke was then 31 years old, while Arthur was 23. Arthur was killed in France six months later, and a third brother, Cecil, died in Flanders in 1917.

In 1915 Edwin Clarke transferred to Lord Strathcona's Horse, and in 1916 he was given a commission in the British army as a Second Lieutenant in the Royal Buckinghamshire Hussars. Research by the historian Philip Walker shows that Clarke subsequently transferred to the Imperial Camel Corps, serving with them in Palestine and the Western Desert. It is possible that he landed this transfer by citing his experience with camels in Gwanda while serving there with the BSAP.

Following the war Clarke went back to Canada, for a while at least, hunting down draft evaders in the wilds of Manitoba for the Royal Canadian Mounted Police. His marriage ended and his wife and children moved to the United States. He remarried and eventually returned to the United Kingdom, where after a thoroughly unconventional life he died in a red-brick semi-detached house in a Southampton suburb in 1955, aged 71.

Edwin Clarke's diary is the unique journal of a young, British colonial police officer in a remote outpost in southern Africa in the early 1900s. Malaria and its effects are a constant theme in the book. Clarke frequently complains of colds and chills, and throughout this diary he reports himself in bed with fever for about one day in ten. The 27-year-old magistrate, Henry Greer, is taken ill with malaria and dies three weeks later, and Greer is the first in a sobering tally of the attrition rate of European settlers through disease, murder, or suicide. A police NCO is reduced to the ranks and burns to death in his bed the following month. James Dalton, an itinerant traveller, turns up at the police camp and begs for food and a bed for the night, before trying to cut his own throat with a pen-knife ("we could see the back of the tongue, but he had missed the jugular…") and stays in Victoria Falls until he is well to be sent with police escort to the asylum in Pretoria. White, a ganger at the mine, kills himself in his cottage.

An unexpected revelation of the diary is how little of Clarke's time as a police officer he actually spent on police duties. Apart from several mounted tours of several days apiece around Hwange, his days on duty seem typically to have been spent parading the native police officers; looking after horses and cleaning his kit; and meeting the trains pulling in at Victoria Falls station. He describes making only one arrest and mentions fewer than a dozen days in court. This apparently left plenty of time to pursue photography and handicrafts, and flirt with young female visitors to Victoria Falls.

Clarke's use of racist language in his diary is offensive by present day standards, but it accurately reflects the typical attitudes of an early twentieth-century white colonist.

Will Sellick
October 2016

Kept by Edwin Gulliver Clarke, Trooper in the British South Africa Police, and being a record of personal events during the year 1906 and also items of interest relating to my life in the B.S.A. Police. Named by natives *Ngadzimbe*.[1]

Sunday 1st January 1906

I spent the morning writing. In the afternoon met the passenger train from the Falls. We celebrated the Scotchman's Xmas last night and at midnight fired a salute. Davis's[2] bolt-head blew out of his rifle and penetrated the water tank.

On the whole today passed off very quietly. I commenced this diary today and intend to make it a compendium for personal and public matters of interest occurring during the year so as to be a record in a sense of my doings, etc., during the years.

Public Holiday in Rhodesia today.

Tuesday 2nd January 1906

Camp routine as usual. Nothing of note occurred. I spent the morning cleaning up my kit. Had a nap in the afternoon. Printed and developed some gaslight prints in the evening.

Wednesday 3rd January 1906

Prepared to leave for Bulawayo to give evidence in a case Rex v C. C. Bennet Contravention of Regulations Re: Cattle. Left on the afternoon train at 4 o'clock for Bulawayo–journey uneventful. Landed in town at 8 o'clock next morning.

---

[1] Possible *Ngazimbi*—"bad blood" (Ndebele)
[2] 720 Frederick Davis

Hilda's[3] birthday. Wrote her the usual wishes etc.

Thursday 4th January 1906

Went to camp. Upon arrival at Bulawayo at 8 o'clock this morning and reported in to old 'Breezy Bill' (S. S. M. Bodle[4]) had some breakfast; found Picaninie[5] Westwood[6] and Duds,[7] also B.S.M. Chalmers in camp down from Hqrs to overhaul the magazine. Saw Lieut Agar[8] and discussed my case with him, he is prosecuting. Attended court at 10am. Waited for our case to be called and as they were some time Bennet and myself adjourned for a drink to the 'Charles' over the road, as soon as we had gone Bennet was called and when we got back we found the magistrate on the point of issuing a warrant for his apprehension. Bennet dismissed insufficient evidence—dined with Bennet and Tpr Ginn[9] who had come in from Inyati at the Queens Hotel.

Amused ourselves during the afternoon; I returned to camp at 6 o'clock having been absent without leave—Breezy wanted to know where the ____ I had been and said he had a ____ good mind to put me on the Reg.[10] He gave me my note and some prisoners to escort back to Wankie. Left town at 8 o'clock and returned to Wankie.

Friday 5th January 1906

Arrived at Malindi at 8 o'clock this morning and saw Mr Beardwell; had a chat with him during the time the train remained in Malindi.

Travelled with Hillier, one of the Guards, in the van as far as Inyati and had breakfast with him: tea made on the engine and German sausage

---

[3] Clarke's younger sister.

[4] Commissioner of the BSAP, Lt Col William Bodle, who had joined the BSAP as a Regimental Sergeant Major.

[5] Piccaninny: slang name for a black child

[6] 138 Sidney Henry Westwood

[7] Possibly 424 George Dudley

[8] Lieutenant W.H. Agar

[9] 446 Edward Ginn

[10] Reg. = Regulations i.e. formally discipline him

and hard-boiled eggs. Arrived in Wankie at 11.40, train an hour late—gave the fellows in camp the news from town.

Wrote the letters for the mail at 3 o'clock this afternoon. Spent the remainder of the afternoon doing odd jobs for myself. Read until bed time.

Saturday 6th January 1906

Spent the day making a bookshelf and cabinet to hold my books and photographic chemicals. Developed 4 plates of the mine[11] during the morning—all four negatives 1/1 plate sizes.

Death of native reported by the colliery boy.

Sunday 7th January 1906

Sunday routine.

I met the train and got the English mail. I received the *Practical Photographer* No. 27 also *Hobbies* and some letters from home. Letter received from Mr Adam Jameson[12] re: the intros I sent him in December. He states he is leaving for England and will see what he can do regarding a billet for me.

December pay arrived, I am 22/- overdrawn. Must put the peg in, this won't do at all.

Monday 8th January 1906

Prisoners on fatigues this morning cleaning up the camp. I saw the Falls train out at 4 o'clock this afternoon.

---

[11] Wankie (now Hwange) coal mine

[12] Adam Jameson (1860-1907) was a Doctor of Medicine who emigrated to Australia in 1884, where he entered politics and became Minister of Lands of Agriculture and leader of the Legislative Council of Western Australia at the time of the Anglo-Boer War. Jameson was appointed in 1902 as Minister for Lands and Agricultre in Milner's Transvaal government after the end of the Anglo-Boer War. He retired from office in 1907 and was killed in a railway accident in the Transvaal the same year.

I spent the evening reading up some special memoranda on photography.

Tuesday 9th January 1906

Nothing worth noting occurred of private interest. Court sat today: 3 natives sentenced for desertion.

Wednesday 10th January 1906

Train from Bulawayo arrived at 11.40 an hour late. Train from Victoria Falls arrived at 8.30, 20 mins late. I wonder when they will stop running toy railways in Rhodesia and run the trains properly.

Received some photographic goods ordered on the 3rd from the Bulawayo Canteen; correct as per invoice.

Thursday 11th January 1906

Printed some postcards for Sissie Gaydon.[13] Toned them in the afternoon, addressed them and wrote descriptions on them in the evening and stamped them ready for the post.

Five of the native police returned from Tshete with 19 deserters from the Wankie Colliery.[14] Stores at station ridden to camp in Scotch cart this morning.

Friday 12th January 1906

Court sat today. Mr Greer[15] the A.N.C.[16] S.J.P.[17] arrived from the Falls. 22 cases tried, all convicted; sentences from 3 weeks or an equivalent fine to 8 months and hard labour given.

---

[13] Sissie Gaydon, whose address is shown in the front of Clarke's diary as being 21 Thames Street, Kingston-on-Thames, Surrey, was Jeanette Gaydon (*pers. comm.* Julie Thorn). Her brother Alfred Bertie Gaydon ("Bertie Gaydon") was only two or three years younger than Clarke. Bertie Gaydon's son was the celebrated spectroscopist Professor 'Dick' (Alfred Gordon) Gaydon.

[14] The colliery at Hwange in Western Zimbabwe was founded in 1899 on the massive coalfield discovered some years earlier.

Report received that 3 natives were killed in the mine last night by a fall of coal. Trprs Watkins[18] and Marryatt[19] viewed the bodies and say they were smashed out of all semblance to human forms.

Lieut Eastwood passed on his way to the Falls to inspect that station.

Saturday 13th January 1906

Mr Greer returned to Matise today. I received a letter from George Errington[20] giving me the news in Salisbury. He is in the C.S.A.'s[21] office now. Nothing to do, he says, and a bob a day extra for doing it. I took some photos in the mine and developed them this afternoon; most of them were not striking successes.

Spent the evening reading. Another native death reported today by the Colliery boy.

Sunday 14th January 1906

Sunday routine.

The train arrived at 9.10 with the English mail. I got two letters and some picture postcards. I spent the evening writing in the Office. I rode out to the Dika and Joseph's Kraal[22] and the Postmaster accompanied me; we found the river in flood and had to wade through it both going and coming back. Our hopeless Posty missed his footing and got a bath whilst crossing, and then got wild because I laughed.

---

15 Henry Francis Greer; originally from Scotland, Greer was a 27-year-old Native Commissioner for Fourth (Matabeleland) District.

16 African Native Commissioner

17 Special Justice of the Peace

18 690 Jesse Thomas Watkins, attested 16 August 1905

19 559 Aubrey Prince Marriott, attested 29 October 1903 and transferred to the Civil Service in 1909. Marriott was born around 1881 in Nottingham, where his father was the managing clerk of a firm of solicitors.

20 282 George Errington, attested for two years on 21 June 1902 and left the BSAP on 20 June 1904.

21 Probably Chief Secretary to the Administrator

22 Kraal: a colonial-era term for an African family homestead

We arrived back in camp at sunset and after I had lent Posty a change we had skoff. He stayed to dinner.

Tuesday 16th January 1906

Usual camp routine. Nothing worthy of note occurred.

Wednesday 17th January 1906

A train each way as usual today. I met both.

Prisoners employed making a garden. Dan Godfrey[23] busy all day in the office. Mr Greer arrived from Matese[24] sick with malaria and went into hospital. Mr Eastwood left for Bulawayo on the afternoon train after inspecting the station.

Thursday 18th January 1906

Mr Greer came out of hospital, said he couldn't stand it. Dan put him up in his room. I wrote my letters for the English mail today.

Friday 19th January 1906

Mail day: two trains as usual. Sgt Godfrey to Bulawayo on duty. Sgt Smith[25] left for the Falls. I prepared some utensils and kit for leaving on patrol to the Gwaai River tomorrow.

Saturday 20th January 1906

Rose at 6.30. Breakfast 8 o'clock. Weighed out and made into packs for 3 donkeys 10 days' rations for myself and N/P[26] Pte Magula and my own native Chalela, also for R17 (Bobbie) and the three donkeys some mealies. This occupied me until 11.30. Allowed three pack saddles to fit the donkey and prepared myself generally for leaving on a ten days

---

[23] 134 William Henry Godfrey, attested 26 May 1901; Godfrey was one of the sergeants at Wankie.

[24] Matetsi

[25] Unidentified: there were four officers called Smith in the Force at this time.

[26] Native policeman

patrol. Dinner 1.30. Wrote a couple of letters for next week's English mail.

Saddled up the three donkeys and started them away at 3.30 this afternoon instructing the Police Boy to proceed to Bongela's Kraal.[27] Saddled up Bobbie at 4.30 after having a cup of tea, and caught up the Police Boy and donkeys. Arrived at Bongela's about an hour after dark and off-saddled there for the night. Cooked some food and had it. Turned in about 11.30.

Sunday 21st January 1906

I got up at dawn—turned the donkeys loose to graze. Prepared some breakfast. Took some photos in and around Bongela's Kraal. Sent a runner to Wankie for my mail. Turned Bobbie loose to graze after the dew was off the grass, read for a little while. Prepared some lunch and had it. Went prospecting along the Locuse[28] River—found "nix ni".[29] Native runner returned from Wankie saying train late and with a note from Marryatt explaining why there was no mail for me. Took some more photos this afternoon. It has just started to rain like mad.

Ate cold cookies[30] and bully[31] for skoff this evening—raining too hard to keep a fire alight. Turned in in a hut Bongela had cleaned for me at 8.30 and went to sleep.

Monday 22nd January 1906

I woke up about 3 o'clock this morning feeling like a big flea-bite. On examination of the hut I found it was infested with vermin. I folded a blanket outside to lay on and curled myself up on it with my greatcoat over me and lay there in the rain till dawn. Woke up this morning and found I had been laying in a puddle of water. Fed the cattle before dawn and at daybreak moved off and trekked for Merriman's Kraal on the

---

[27] A homestead about nine miles from the police station.
[28] Lokuzi River
[29] *Niks nie* = nothing (Afrikaans)
[30] Probably *vetkoek* = deep-fried, unsweetened bread dough (Afrikaans)
[31] Bully = bully beef or corned beef

Inyatie River. At about 12 noon I offsaddled for the heat of midday, the sun having come out again, tried to get dry and cooked some breakfast etc.

At 3.30 we moved on again and landed at Merriman's just after dark. Came on to rain again at sunset and rained all night. I had a tin of bully for skoff and got under the blankets shortly afterwards. Merriman offered me one of his huts to sleep in but I prefer rain to vermin and I declined and lay in the rain all night again, sopped through of course.

Tuesday 23rd January 1906

Everything sopping wet this morning, saddled up at dawn and trekked to Jacob's Kraal, arriving at 10 o'clock am. Off-saddled here for a few hours; the rain ceased and the sun came out and we dried and had some food. Saddled up again and trekked as far as Big Fley,[32] halfway to Dingaan's Kraal.[33]

Soon after leaving Jacob's I shot a duiker—missed him twice and then lost him in long grass out of which he shortly walked when I hit him with a hollow-nose and dropped him in his tracks. Halted the donkeys and placed the carcase on one of them. Arrived at Big Fley at sunset and off-saddled there for the night, skinned, cleaned and cut up the duiker.

It started raining again in torrents and altho' I tried to eat some liver I found more grit than anything else so had to leave it; spent the night trying to dodge the rain.

Wednesday 24th January 1906

Saddled up as soon as it was light enough to do and trekked to Dingaan's; it stopped raining at about 9 o'clock and the sun came out about eleven. We arrived at Dingaan's about 9.30 and off-saddled there for midday. I gave a leg of duiker to Dingaan and cooked the two haunches for my own consumption; the rest I gave to Magula and

---

[32] *Vlei.* (Afrikaans) a marshy wetland
[33] Dingane, a chieftaincy near Hwange

Chalela. Made some notes in my pocket book. Came on to rain again at 3.30 approx and continued for two days. I moved into the Kraal and Dingaan made his natives build me a shelter—I slept dry tonight. Had some duiker at 7.30. Read notes on enlarging for an hour or so and then went to sleep.

Thursday 25th January 1906

Saddled up at daybreak and after a cup of coffee got on the road again for Hawthorne's Farm. Saw a duiker but did not get a shot at him. Off-saddled at Jackalasse's Kraal on the road for breakfast and to graze the cattle. Saddled up again and trekked to Big tree outspan where off-saddled again to have some lunch. Tried to take some photos—saddled up again and trekked to Hawthorne's passing Deckerts en route. Remained at Hawthorne's the night.

Friday 26th January 1906

As it rained all day I remained at Hawthorne's until tomorrow morning. Colonel Chester Masters,[34] Commandant-General B.S.A.P., passed through Wankie on his way to Vict. Falls.

Saturday 27th January 1906

Saddled up at daybreak this morning and proceeded to Deckerts; saw Mr D and got some particulars on a native from him, rode on again as far as Big tree outspan, where I off-saddled for a few hours rest at midday. Saddled up again and proceeded on to Dingaan's Kraal, arriving at that place at sunset.

I shot a steinbuck and two guinea fowl between Big Tree and Dingaan's. Country passed through was mostly forest and in several places I saw recent spoor of elephants and had hopes of coming up with them but was unsuccessful. It has left off raining and is fine now.

---

[34] Lieutenant-Colonel Richard Chester-Master, Resident Commissioner of Southern Rhodesia 1905-1908.

Sunday 28th January 1906

No rain this morning. Saddled up at sawn and trekked to Big Fley, off-saddling there for midday. Saddled up again and trekked past Jacob's to Merriman's Kraal where we remained the night.

Trekking during the day through forest broken in places with grass and marshy fleys. Very monotonous travelling and the trek was devoid of anything of interest. Came on to rain at about 2 o'clock pm and continued all night.

Monday 29th January 1906

Left Merriman's at daybreak and trekked to Bongela's, halting for midday at Big Tree outspan. Arrived at Bongela's at sunset. Shot a bush heron at Big Tree. Still raining.

Tuesday 30th January 1906

It left off raining during the night. Saddled up and saw the donkeys started at daybreak and then rode straight into Wankie, arriving in time for breakfast—got several letters. Heard that Mr Greer was in hospital with blackwater fever.[35] N/P Magulu, Chalela, the pack donkeys etc arrived at midday in camp. Squared up generally and got dry clothes etc.

Wednesday 31st January 1906

The usual train each way today. Camp routine. Nothing unusual occurred. I was employed cleaning up kit after my patrol all day.

Thursday 1st February 1906

Camp routine as usual. Wrote my letters for the English mail. Nothing worthy of note occurred.

---

[35] Malarial haemolysis, which turns the urine reddish-brown or black

Friday 2nd February 1906

Mr Greer reported taken a turn for the better. Mr Jackson and his wife[36] arrived from [Fort] Usher (sister and brother-in-law of Greer's). Nothing unusual occurred. I feel a bit seedy, so does Watkins.

Saturday 3rd February 1906

Mr Greer died this morning about 2.30am and was buried at sunset. Watkins and myself in bed all day—fever. Poor old 'Ginger', our pet mule, succumbed to colic at 7 o'clock this evening.

Sunday 4th February 1906

Marryatt met the mail train and got the English mails. Pay arrived from town. Watkins and myself still in bed. Sunday routine in camp, heavy rains this afternoon.

Monday 5th February 1906

Watkins pretty bad. I feel better and got up at midday. Sgt Godfrey to Bulawayo on duty. Camp routine as per usual. N/P Cpl Majane left for Bulawayo a prisoner this afternoon for drunk and neglect of duty, to be dealt with by O.C. Troop Capt. Tomlinson.[37]

Tuesday 6th February 1906

Nothing of note occurred. Watkins a bit better. I am nearly alright again. Marryatt only—no ease up for duty.

Wednesday 7th February 1906

Sgt Godfrey returned from Bulawayo. Watkins worse again.

Returned to duty today.

---

[36] Hugh Gower Jackson, whose wife was Martha Lawson Greer of Natal. Jackson was a Native Commissioner in Matabeleland and was assistant magistrate for Bulawayo district.

[37] Alfred James Tomlinson, who served as Lieutenant-Colonel with the Rhodesia Native Regiment in East Africa during the First World War

Thursday 8th February 1906

Usual camp routine.

Mr and Mrs Jackson left to return to Usher. I wrote my letters for the English mail and posted them. Nothing worthy of special note occurred.

Friday 9th February 1906

We heard this morning that Mr Agar is coming up here to take charge of the station as soon as the quarters for him have been built. Two trains as usual today.

Maj.-Gen. Baden-Powell[38] passed through on his way to the Falls. Actg R.S.M. Hoaten arrived from Bulawayo to drill Volunteers. Had dinner with us this evening. Bill Hoaten put me through my drill when I was a Rookie in the police and he was Sgt and drill instr. Later he took over as instructor to the S.R.V.s[39] and was transferred to their permanent staff.

Saturday 10th February 1906

Prisoners working down at the new range cleaning off the bush. Nothing of note occurred—usual camp routine.

Sunday 11th February 1906

Mail day. I met the train and got the mails. Two papers only for me.

Monday 12th February 1906

Nothing of note occurred. Bill Hoaten left on this afternoon's train for Bulawayo.

---

[38] Maj Gen Robert Baden-Powell, founder of the Boy Scouts
[39] Southern Rhodesia Volunteers: the Rhodesian territorial force.

Tuesday 13th February 1906

Usual camp routine. Nothing worthy of mention occurred.

Wednesday 14th February 1906

Usual camp duties. Two on station duty today.

Watkins, Marryatt and Dan Godfrey went to search for a native early this morning in the 'wee small hours'. Didn't find him though, unluckily.

Thursday 15th February 1906

Wrote my letters for the mail tomorrow. Nothing worthy of note occurred today.

Friday 16th February 1906

Outgoing English mail today. I was in charge of a fatigue at the station riding grain and 60 bales of hay up to the camp and general stores etc for the station. Trps Marryatt left with N/P Pte [illegible] on patrol to the Gwaai river and vicinity.

Saturday 17th February 1906

Native Nashu arrested for trying to obtain liquor on a forged note. I toned and fixed some prints in the morning. Had a nap in the afternoon. Letter received from Colonel Trueman by local train today.

Sunday 18th February 1906

Letter received from Colonel Trueman, Sis Gaydon, Cyril,[40] People from Cyril, letter from father.

I met the train from Bulawayo at 9.50 (40 mins late) and got the mail for the camp.

---

[40] Clarke's younger brother Cyril

Hobbies received from Dawsons. Went for a walk in the afternoon; took Tpr and Tiny with me;[41] collected a few beetles to take home for Mr Elliman's collection. Wrote some letters during the evening to Mother, Cyril and Hilda. Also Bert Gaydon.

Monday 19th February 1906

Rose at sunrise, weighed out and made into packs 10 days' rations for myself, N/P Pte Dabane, Horse R17 (Bobbie) and 3 pack donkeys. Stables 7.30 till 8 o'clock—8 o'clock breakfast—wrote two letters after breakfast for next mail.

I feel a bit dicky this morning—another bad cold I fancy. I left on patrol for Geese[42] Farm, Pandamitanga,[43] The Border Road, Klass Africa's Farm[44] and Matthasen's[45] Farm. Intended to trek as far as Jackies Kraal but owing to the old road being overgrown I missed the road and we landed on the bank of the Deka River about 5 miles NW of Jackies, where I decided to remain the night and proceed on to Jackies next morning. I sent Dabane along to a kraal about ½ a mile up the river to root out a native to show me the shortest road to Jackies in the morning which he did. Feeling seedy and feverish. Turned in, taking 20 grains of quinine and a stiff tot of dop and bit of skoff.

Tuesday 20th February 1906

I had the horse and donkeys fed before dawn and at dawn saddled up and leaving the Deka we trekked across country to Jackies. The path running over kopjes of the way—arrived at Jackies about 7 o'clock. There I commandeered the services of another native to accompany me to Geese Farm as I am new to this road and don't intend to miss it

---

[41] Clarke's retriever dogs

[42] Giese Farm

[43] Pandamatenga

[44] Klaas Afrika was a mixed-race man who had been one of the earliest European settlers in Zimbabwe; he worked as a guide for game hunters, and married one of the daughters of Lobengula.

[45] Matthysen – probably the same family recorded in *Rhodesia's Pioneer Women* by Jessie M. Lloyd as living on 'Matabele' Wilson's farm near Bulawayo in 1894

again. The road onto Bomboos[46] is where I off saddled about twelve o'clock until 3 o'clock during the heat of midday, also to graze my horse and the donkeys.

Bomboos is a large fley mostly with the Deka river running down on e side and surrounded on all sides by hills; it is abundantly stocked with game of all sorts. As soon as we off-saddled I lay down as riding had upset me considerably, especially my back. Later on after saddling up at 3 o'clock and when we had been trekking for about on an hour we saw 4 hd of sable antelope in front of us but did not shoot. We off-saddled for the night at a river named the Dulelo.

Wednesday 21st February 1906

The night's rest has done me good and I feel much more like myself this morning, but weak—I suppose want of food, the quinine etc would account for that. I must shoot a buck if I can manage to hold my rifle steady to make some soup. Saddled up at sunrise and left for Little Tom,[47] where I intend to off saddle for midday.

I find Tom is nearer than I expected, so passed it and trekked as far as I could before it got too hot. About two miles beyond Tom whilst crossing a small spruit I saw a couple of water buck on the opposite bank, and nipped off my horse and potted one of them. I found on getting over to him that I had hit him through the neck and broken it, dropping him instantly. I cut his throat to bleed him and then the boys skinned him. I made some soup with a bit of the sirloin, the rest I cut off and divided equally amongst the donkey packs, also taking the horns. We mucked about—2 o'clock again as far as Little Tom, where we spent the night.

Thursday 22nd February 1906

Saddled up at daybreak and trekked to Geese Farm. I feel alright almost today—I think my cold or chill has run its 3-day course and tomorrow

---

[46] Bambusi
[47] Now part of the Hwange National Park

will see me all O.K. again. The country we passed through was firstly forest, and after that splendid, big, undulating fleys all the way to Geese place, with water everywhere. During the trek I saw an eland bull, a herd of tsessebe, a big sable antelope, two reed buck and several duiker and steenbuck. I did not attempt to shoot anything as I have plenty of meat with me (the waterbuck must weigh about 800lbs) .

Arrived at Geese Farm about 1 o'clock and after off-saddling I lay down until evening. Geese[48] has gone to Klass Africa's place on biz. and will be back at sunset. We had some dinner of waterbuck and vegetables, yarned for a while and then turned in. Mosquitoes galore.

Friday 23rd February 1906

Got up soon after daybreak and saw my horse and donkeys get their mealies; after that Dubane groomed Bobbie. Walked about the place till breakfast time at 8 o'clock. Spent the morning with Mr Giese in his sitting room examining his collection of butterflies, moths, beetles and other natural history subjects. Also saw his collection of guns and sporting rifles—he has the nattiest sporting carbine I have seen in Rhodesia.

Lunch 1.30. Went on a tour of inspection around the mealie lands and melon and pumpkin plantations; ate well—Mr Giese. Took some photos in the mealie avenue and of the Deka river etc. The Deka has its source about 200 yds above Mr Giese's house and is fed from springs. It flows into the Gwaai river near where the Gwaai river joins the Zambezi. Dinner—read of some records of big game until 9 o'clock— listened to Mr G yarning about the '93 and '96 Rebellions[49] till 10.30:

---

[48] Albert Giese (1865-1938) German-born prospector and the discoverer of the coalfield at Hwange in 1894. Giese was educated at Hersfeld and Fulda Gymnasium and joined the Natal Mounted Police in 1884 at the age of 19. In 1889 he joined the Bechuanaland Border Police, resigning in 1892 to prospect in the Tati region. Giese traded in partnership with H. G. Robins, whose nearby farm forms the nucleus of Hwange National Park, and became a British citizen in 1935. Clarke spells Giese's name Geese until the following day's entry—presumably corrected by Giese himself.

[49] Rebellions of the Ndebele and Shona peoples against colonial rule.

turned in. More mosquitoes—this place is infested with them, they spread fever.

Saturday 24th February 1906

I saddled up my horse at 7 o'clock this morning and, taking N/P Pte Dabane with me, visited Klass Africa's and Matthasen's farms, returning to Giese's place the same day, distance 40 miles approx. For the first few miles the going was very bad and consisted of boggy fleys into which Bobbie sank up to his knees several times and necessitated my dismounting and leading him. I arrived at Klass's about 12 noon and stayed about a quarter of an hour, I then proceeded on to Matthasen's, arriving about 1.30. I was invited to off-saddle and did so for about an hour or so.

These people are Dutch, and the family consists of Matthesen, his wife, two grown-up daughters and about half a dozen girls of various ages and sizes and a son about 19 years old. They all sat round the room and stared at me as if I was some sort of curio or wild man of Borneo or something of the sort. Altho' they could speak English I could not get any conversation beyond monosyllables out of any of them excepting the son who had nothing to talk of except the chances for and against the Barotsi's army.[50] I proceeded back to G's place and about an hour before I got there it was quite dark and we had to go by guesswork and Bobbie's instinct, as the path was difficult to follow by daylight, and impossible to do so after dark. However, we landed back at Giese's about 8 o'clock and upon my arrival G shouted up the dinner which we had and then we sat yarning and reading until about 11.30.

I shall be free of mosquitoes tonight and able to sleep: Giese has dug out an old mosquito net from somewhere, so here goes for six hours' shut-eye.

---

[50] The Barotse are a nation living in the region of the floodplain of the Lozi River in what is now Zambia, Botswana, Zimbabwe and Namibia. There was tension in 1906 as a result of the British administration abolishing the traditional system of serfdom upon which cultivation of the Lozi lands had depended, and it may be that this—with memories of the Chimurenga only a few years old—gave rise to rumours of rebellion among the white settlers.

Sunday 25th February 1906

I got my six hours sleep all O.K. last night and lay in until 8 o'clock this morning. Got up for breakfast at 8.30. Cleaned my rifle, read a history of Rhodesia—the first on Rhodesia I have seen; it is not very accurate, and on a lot of subjects Mr Giese was kind enough to tell me absolute facts where the author was at fault, Mr Giese having been an eye witness of most of the incidents mentioned.

Lunch—read some more of the History. Started raining in torrents about 3.30, and is in for a wet night, I think. I shall remain here tomorrow if it rains as I cannot afford to get another chill on top of the one I have just got rid of. Dinner. I sat yarning with Mr Giese until bed time. Turned in at 10.30 and slept like a top until 3.30, when I awoke to hear the dogs barking and got up to see what it was, and heard a lion about a mile away I should say, the dogs chased him; I went back to bed again.

Monday 26th February 1906

Rose at daybreak, saw my cattle fed. Walked about till 8.30. Breakfast. Saw the packs made up again ready to leave after dinner. Chatted for a while with Mr Giese—we went round the mealie lands with shotguns. Giese bagged a brace of pheasants and I shot two guinea fowl. Dinner or lunch. Pack up my donkeys and started them off about 2.30. I followed and caught them up about an hour afterwards. I saw fresh spoor of a lion on the road about a mile out from G's place, the one that the dogs chased probably. I kept a sharp look-out for him but did not see him. Trekked as far as Tom where we outspanned for the night— had some skoff. Turned in shortly after dark. Heard a lion about 2.30 a.m. Banked up the fires, cocked my rifle and sat up; by his roaring he appeared to be going away from me so I went to sleep and never heard him again.

Tuesday 27th February 1906

Fed Bobbie and the donkeys before dawn. Saddled up at dawn and moved off just as the top of the sun showed over the horizon. Trekked as far as the first water this side of Little Tom and off-saddled there for lunch during the heat of midday and to graze my cattle etc. Saddled up again about 2.30 and trekked to Bomboos.

Just before reaching Bomboos I saw some zebra and got off to have a look at them at as close quarters as I could get; I rode Bobbie to within 250 yards of them and getting off, crawled on hands and knees to within a 100 yds of them and lay and watched them. After while I sneezed and they tried to get upwind and as I was nearly upwind of them they came galloping by within a hundred yards of me and I then saw that there were tsessebe with them. I took a pot shot at the tsessebe, picking out a bull, but missed him. Off-saddled at Bomboos and remained the night.

Wednesday 28th February 1906

Mosquitoes galore here. Saddled up at daybreak and went to look for the tsessebe I say yesterday. Could not find them so made a circle skirting the hills round Bomboos, I saw a tsessebe bull and his cow and shot him, hitting him in the near shoulder and fetching him to his knees; a bullet in the brain finished him. Returned to the outspan and fetched two donkeys and loaded them up with the meat, I then saddled up again after some skoff and trekked to Jackies Kraal, arriving at sunset. I remained here the night.

Thursday 1st March 1906

Saw the donkeys saddled up and started them off; I then saddled up and accompanied by the two dogs, Trpr[51] and Tiny, rode straight into Wankie, leaving N/P Pte Dubane and my own native Chalela and the pack donkeys to follow on at an easy pace. I arrived in Wankie at 12

---

[51] i.e. Trooper

noon and reported to Dan Godfrey the N.C.O.[52] i/c[53] here. Lunch—wrote to Mother, Cyril, W. Hughes, Watsons and Tylars, and sent two P.P.C.s[54] for tomorrow's outgoing English mail.

At 3.30 the boys and donkeys arrived in camp. [illegible] 5 o'clock I dashed out skoff (mealie meal and salt to my boy and Dabane). Dinner. Read some papers that had arrived during my absence. Turned in, slept like a top till 6.30.

Heard from Watkins that Nashu, one of the prisoners, had escaped and been recaught during the time I had been away, for which he got sjambokked.[55]

Friday 2nd March 1906

Met the train from Bulawayo. Cooked the meals today and took over cook until Sunday week.

Met the train from the Falls; Miss Lily Blakewell[56] and Miss Rose Hobson were on board. I didn't speak to them. Spent the evening reading, writing.

Marryatt in bed with malaria, only a shift's dose.

Saturday 3rd March 1906

Rose at 7.00. Cooked the breakfast (liver and bacon). Saw the horses groomed. Gave the police boys and prisoners their mealie meal etc. Breakfast 8.30.

Camp routine till lunch at 1 o'clock. Cooked the lunch.

Sent my boy to the store for soap, tobacco, matches and groceries for the mess. Had a nap for an hour or so. Cooked dinner and made a pie. Gave the camp boys their skoff. Spent the evening reading for a while.

---

[52] N.C.O.: Non-commissioned officer

[53] i/c: a British Army abbreviation signifying 'in command'

[54] P.P.C.: picture postcard

[55] i.e. beaten with a *sjambok*, a leather whip traditionally made from hippo hide

[56] Possibly the daughter of a Rhodesia Railways engine-driver named Blakewell.

Developed films exposed on patrol and found that the shutter hadn't worked properly and let in light: result, 2 negatives any good out of 24 exposures. Quoted poetry.

Turned in at 10.30. I heard today that Joe Tedder[57] had purchased his discharge that Cpl Pim[58] has been reduced to the ranks for absent from duty whilst actg. C.S.[59]; that Earle[60] and Hoad[61] are getting a medical board, and also that Staff S.M.[62] Baker[63] has been smashed to the ranks for drunk and making a beast of himself at a cricket-match in Bulawayo—charged with conduct prejudicial to the good conduct of the Corps. Rats! Poor old Willie, they have been looking for a chance to smash you for a long time.

Sunday 4th March 1906

Watkins met the English mail train on its arrival at 9.30, and got the letters. I got 2 postcards from Sissie Gaydon, a letter from Cyril and *Hobbies* and the *Practical Photographer* No. 28 from Dawsons.

Sunday routine (i.e. kill time). Printed some postcards, cooked the meals etc. Went for a walk in the afternoon and collected some butterflies and beetles for Mr Elliman. Dinner at 7 o'clock. Wrote two letters. Turned in 9.30.

Monday 5th March 1906

Nothing worthy of note occurred: camp routine as usual. I cooked all meals. Watkins saw Falls train for Bwayo out at 4 o'clock. I sent one dozen mounted photos of the mine down to *Incani* Woods at the Bar to

---

[57] 290 Joseph William Tedder, attested 21 June 1902

[58] 120 William Charles Pim, attested 25 October 1900. Pim was burnt to death a month later, on 12 April 1906.

[59] C.S.: Colour Sergeant

[60] 94 Herbert Earle, attested 30 July 1899

[61] 664 Aubrey George Hoad, attested just ten months earlier on 31 May 1905; he was discharged as medically unfit on 31 March 1904.

[62] Staff S.M.: Staff Sergeant-Major

[63] 460 William James Baker, attested 31 March 1903; Baker transferred to the Civil Service in 1909.

sell at 3/- each. I spent the evening reading and went to bed early. Heard today that the Skipper[64] has passed his law exam successfully.

Tuesday 6th March 1906

Nothing occurred today. Camp routine.

Native prisoners working down at the new range.

Wednesday 7th March 1906

A passenger train arrived from Town at 10.40 and another from the Falls at 3.10. Marryatt met both trains. Case of arson reported from the railway location, culprit arrested and put in trunk.[65] I wrote to McLochlin[66], Bwyo Canteen, for 3 chisels, a small iron smooth plane, dovetail saw, 2 ft of strip , packet of ½ in. screws, 6lbs hyper,[67] 6 spools for the No. 2 Brownie Kodak and the chassis.

Nothing worthy of note occurred, the same old everyday humdrum camp existence as usual.

Thursday 8th March 1906

Rose before sunrise and went out with shotgun to look for [illegible] and found none. Camp routine.

Wrote my letters in the evening for the outgoing English mail. Sgt Cooke repaired my saddlery this morning for me.

Friday 9th March 1906

Train from town 10.40. Train from Falls 3.10. Farrier Sgt Smith arrived from Bulawayo. Sgt Dan Godfrey left on this afternoon's train to give evidence in a case in Bulawayo. Left me in charge as Senior Trooper.

---

[64] *Skipper* is a police slang term for sergeant—presumably this refers to Sergeant Godfrey passing a law examination to allow him to pass to the next rank.

[65] *Tronk*: Afrikaans, 'prison'.

[66] Probably 332 William George McLoghlin, attested 24 July 1902.

[67] Probably 'hypo'— sodium hyposulphite—used for developing photographic prints.

Smith shod the horses. I feel a bit seedy; touch of fever, turned in early and took some quinine.

Saturday 10th March 1906

Arrested a man named Forsyth for drunk and creating a disturbance, infringing pass ordinance laws, and forgery. Raided the compound at 3.30 a.m. and got several natives on [illegible] charges. Wrote a letter to Geo Errington, Salisbury. Issued 48 passes to natives. Camp routine. Prisoners on fatigues, cleaning up camp. I spent the evening reading till 9.30. Turned in and took 20 more grains of quinine.

Sunday 11th March 1906

Mail received from Bulawayo and England. I got a letter from Mother and one from Father, Hilda and Cyril and the *People* from Cyril, a p.p.c. from Sis and *Hobbies* from Dawsons. Sunday routine. I went for a walk in the afternoon and spent the evening mounting photos.

Monday 12th March 1906

Nothing worthy of special note occurred. Camp routine as usual. Saddler Sgt Cooke left for Bulawayo repairing our saddlery. Wrote a long letter to Sis Gaydon describing the Pandamitanga patrol etc.

Cooke gave me some needles, thread and wax and leather etc. I made two collars for Trooper and Tiny in the afternoon.

Tuesday 13th March 1906

Cleaned up generally and saw the boys scrub out the rooms. Spent the afternoon serving subpoenas and summonses for court tomorrow. I borrowed a pair of scissors and hair clippers from the Postmaster (Portingale) and Watkins cut my hair for me.

Wednesday 14th March 1906

Mr Fuller the acting Native Commissioner arrived from Matise. Mr Carey the magistrate arrived from Bulawayo. Court sat, all cases tried conviction secured. I went down to the mine compound and fetched up 18 native witnesses.

Received 3 chisels, a plane, dovetail saw, pkt of screws, 6lbs hypo, the chassis and 6 spools for no. 2 Brownie also ½ lb carbonate of soda from McLochlin this afternoon. I spent this evening posting up this diary from odd memorandum in notebooks. Sgt Armfield[68] and prisoners arrived from the Falls to attend court tomorrow. Turned in at 10.40p.m.

Thursday 15th March 1906

Rose at 7.30 washed, shaved etc. Breakfast at 8 o'clock. Court sat again today and cases from the Falls tried. Gave my boy some washing to do and the stirrup irons and bit of my saddle to clean. Scrubbed my bandolier and cleaned it up again. Did odd jobs that required doing around the camp. Wrote to Mother and Cyril. Posted my budget to Sis. I repaired my saddle-bag and a pair of boots. Sharpened some tools; set some butterflies and cured a skin also scraped the waterbuck horns. Spent the evening taking it in turns to sing songs. Went to bed at 10.30.

Friday 16th March 1906

We all overslept this morning and Watson, one of the carpenters from the mine, came up and caught us all in bed. Watson and myself went down to the range to fix the new targets and their carriages etc, returned for lunch at 1p.m. Sent down to the Bar in the morning for half a dozen 'Bass'[69] and Watson and I swallowed them between us, it being hot and thirsty working on the range. N/P Pte Simwarara and 2 prisoners working in butts.

One of us to go to Bulawayo with a batch of prisoners committed for trial and Marryatt and myself tossed for it. I won, so he went, leaving at 4 o'clock by train this afternoon. Sgt Armfield and the two native police from Victoria Falls returned to that station on this morning's train.

---

[68] 85 Archie Seward Armfield, attested 24 May 1899. Armfield died at Canada Farm near Ypres in Belgium in October 1917, a Second Lieutenant in the 2nd Bttn Irish Guards
[69] Bass bottled ale

Watson stayed to lunch. We went down to the range again at 2.30, but it started to rain in torrents and we had to make a bolt for it. I was catching butterflies for Mr Elliman's collection beyond the 600 yds mark and had to sprint for it; I think I managed to do the 600 yds in about as quick time as I have managed since leaving Bulawayo at the latter end of last footer season. Got sopped before reaching camp, couldn't see very well owing to the downpour beating in my face and ran into trees twice—got a black eye from one of them. Changed into dry clothes—set the butterflies I had caught. Cooked tonight's dinner—issued the grain for the horses, mule and donkeys. Gave the camp boys their mealie meal. Printed and developed some gaslight prints—views of colliery ordered by *Incansi*[70] Woods. Posted up my diary. Turned in at 12.30p.m. Rain set for the night.

Saturday 17th March 1906

Rose at 7 o'clock. Dan went to investigate a complaint laid by pumper[71] re natives refusing to work, natives arrested and later worked for the government with pick and shovel on the range under persuasion from myself. I prepared the breakfast. My boy Chalela reports sick—fever. 15 grains quinine and one phenacetin, and told him to keep himself warm and lie down. Went down to the range to superintend natives at work. Caught some butterflies for Mr E's collection. Told the natives to cease work at 1.15p.m. Returned to camp and saw lunch dished up etc. Lunch 1.40p.m. Set the butterflies I had caught. Planed down some ¼ in deals for use—made two store boxes in the afternoon for the butterflies. Cooked dinner. Wrote to Colonel Freeman or rather continued the letter I started last night. Amused myself during the evening setting butterflies and transferring others to the new store boxes. This occupied me until 10.30. After dinner Dan Godfrey and Watkins strolled down to the Bar and returned at 10.40. Posted up the day's events as above. Turned in at 11 o'clock p.m.

---

70 *iNcansi* = a sleeping mat made from split reeds (Ndebele). Later on Clarke refers to Woods as Inceni Woods. Woods appears to have managed the hotel in Wankie.
71 Pumper: staffed the pumps in Wankie Colliery

Sunday 18th March 1906

English mail day. Train arrived at 10.45. I got the following mail—postcard from Sissie, letter from Cyril, also the *People* and *Chesham Examiner*, letter and booklet from Houghtons, and *Hobbies*. Rose at 7.30, prepared breakfast. Dan Godfrey and Watkins went to the station to meet the train which was over an hour late. Trpr Marryatt returned from Bulawayo.

I painted the new office table; dipped my retrievers in a strong solution of Jeyes Fluid and water to kill the ticks they pick up in the long grass. Wrote a letter. Prepared the lunch. Took some photos in the afternoon. Reading mail.

I heard from natives today that there are some ancient ruins near Lecasi[72] Siding in a fair state of preservation. I shall go out on the 1st opportunity and photograph them. Read during the afternoon, turned in at 9.30. Raining in torrents all night.

Monday 19th March 1906

Rose at 8 o'clock this morning. Breakfast at 8.30. Watkins takes over cook for the week. I walked down to the range after breakfast in company with Marryatt. We stayed down there all the morning superintending the work being done etc. Sgt Godfrey and Watkins strolled down just before lunch. Fonseca the Surface Boss from the mine was also down. I spent the afternoon painting a box etc. Marryatt was at the range, Dan in the 'Village' and Watkins in the office. Dan Godfrey went down to the hotel to skoff and after we had had our skoff at 7.30, Watkins and Marryatt also went down and I spent the evening in the office writing letters. Turned in at 11.30.

Wire received from Falls stating Nashu the native who had escaped recently from here has been recaptured.

---

[72] Lukozi

Tuesday 20th March 1906

Quarterly musketry competition held. Sgt Godfrey and *Incansi* Woods rode out to Locasi to see the ruins there and the Doctor (Dr Kennedy) with them. Marriot is looking after the Hotel for *Incansi*.

I printed some photos and postcards and went down to the range during the morning. Lunch 1.30p.m. Fixed prints and postcards in the afternoon and read for a while; did some writing. Came on to rain about 3.30 and continued until dark. Printed and developed gaslight papers in the evening—hung them up to dry and turned in at 11.30p.m.

Wednesday 21st March 1906

Quarterly musketry competition finishes today and results appear in Orders a month today. Marriott on station duty; usual two trains today. I felt seedy this morning so got the thermometer and found my temperature 103.2 Turned in and piled greatcoats and started the old system of quinine and perspiration. Took some more quinine at sunset.

Tpr Waters[73] arrived from Vict Falls at 3.10 and went back on a goods train at 9.30.

Thursday 22nd March 1906

Felt much better today so got up and pottered about in camp. I shifted my quarters to another part of the room away from windows as I put yesterday's indisposition down to a chill caught by the draught between two windows when hot.

Came over queer again about 5 o'clock p.m. and got to bed again— more perspiring and 15 grs quinine, temperature 103.4.

Autumn season commences in Rhodesia from today till June 22nd.

Friday 23rd March 1906

Remained in bed all day.

---

[73] 157 Thomas William Waters, attested 18 June 1901

Temperature	9.30am	103
"	12 noon	104.2
"	6 p.m.	103

Diet 1 glass of milk

Saturday 24th March 1906

In bed all day. Temperature reduced to 98 this morning; 101.4 at 12 noon; normal at 6p.m.

Diet Brand's Extract of Beef and soup in the evening. N/P/Pte Siabuta had a long strip of hippo hide from me today to make me a stick.

Sunday 25th March 1906

Got up for breakfast and dressed in flannels; mooned about in camp in the shade all day feeling pretty weak. Dan went down to the station to meet the Mail train in at 9.10 a.m and sent up my mail by the police boy Simwauri. Letters received from Sis Gaydon and mother. I wrote to Sis Gaydon as I could not do much else today and it was a good opportunity to reply to her letter.

Watkins and Marryatt down at the range all the morning. Also addressed p.p.c.s to Bert, Sis, Winnie and Dorothy Gaydon. Spent the afternoon reading papers which arrived by the mail today. Wrote for a short while this evening and then went to bed early. I have had my temperature at normal all day and with the exception of a bit of a headache alright again.

Monday 26th March 1906

I am alright today and took over Cook for the week from Marryatt. Prepared meals and did odd jobs during the morning. Printed 14 postcards of the following subjects this afternoon:

The Devil's Cataract Rapids
Inyati 96 Memorial

Cricket Match at Gwanda
B.S.A.P. N.P. Gwanda
Native Women in a Kraal below Gwaai River
C. J. Cooke's House, Gwanda
Horse Lines the Camp Gwanda
Geelong from Kopje
Native curing duikah skin
B.S.A.P. transport at Geelong Camp
Native exhibiting with an assegai
Saddle and Arms Inspection Gwanda

Read the overseas mail, prepared dinner. Wrote a letter during the evening and turned in a 9.30 p.m. Mr Lear has started a library here so we in Wankie will be a bit better off for reading matter.

Tuesday 27th March 1906

Rose at 7.35. Cooked breakfast which we ate at 8.30. Camp routine as per usual. Wrote two letters and mended some equipment during the morning. Had a suspected native lunatic handed over to us today by the butcher McLaren. Lunch.

I toned postcards and spent the remainder of the afternoon reading. Dinner 7.30. Dan, Marryatt and Watkins have gone down to raid the compounds. I spent the evening reading and writing etc and turned in at 10 o'clock. Nothing unusual occurred today.

Wednesday 28th March 1906

I rose at 7.30 and prepared breakfast. Met the train from Town at 11 o'clock–20 minutes late. Wrote to Cyril enclosing stamps and returning Sissie's letter. Lunch 1.30. Met train from the Falls in the afternoon at 3.10. Printed some postcards for Portingale and prepared dinner. Evening stables 5.00 till 6. Dinner 6.30. Spent the evening reading. I turned in at 9.30. N/P Pte Lianiatchela to Bulawayo sick.

Thursday 29th March 1906

Camp routine as usual. Nothing unusual occurred. I wrote some letters during the course of the day for the English mail tomorrow and sent Chalela down to the post with them also the ½ doz postcards for Portingale which I had toned etc this morning. Cleaned my rifle and put my saddle in dubbin etc.

I spent the evening reading Jany. and Feby. nos of the London.[74] Turned in at 10.30 p.m.

Friday 30th March 1906

Outgoing mail day. Tpr Marryatt Station duty usual two trains one up and one down to Town. Lieut Agar's horse arrived on the train this morning a little Tpr: bay stallion about 14 hds high and of a useful build. I spent the morning and a portion of the afternoon converting two strips of hippo hide into a riding crop and walking stick respectively. Varnished and finished them etc. Spent the remainder of the afternoon reading. Dan is sick (fever) and has turned in. A case of assault reported by the Colliery Co. against D. McKenzie, a miner. Spent the evening writing and mounting photos.

Saturday 31st March 1906

Received this morning from Bulawayo K Troop Canteen goods as order:

2 lbs Capetown Medium Tobacco	7/-
12 pks cigarette papers @ 1d	1/-
1 pkt matches	6d
1 pkt B.S.A.P. note paper	1/9d
1 box crested police cards and envelopes	1/6
Total	11/9 plus carriage

---

[74] i.e. January and February editions of the *Illustrated London News*

Dan Godfrey ill in bed fever at present but suspected Blackwater. Marriot went to the station and rode Bobbie down before breakfast this morning to send off a consignment of goods to Matise. Watkins exercised Mr Agar's horse for an hour before breakfast. I prepared breakfast.

After breakfast I amused myself constructing a cleaning kit box which occupied me till 3.30 p.m. with an hour interval for lunch at 1 o'clock. Marryatt spent the afternoon down at Meikle Bros Store[75] assisting Mr Lear the manager with his books etc. I wrote a letter in the afternoon. Case of assault reported by a native against R. Phillips, Pumper here. Summons applied for.

I purchased 4 stripes of hippo hide with the intention of making sjamboks and riding switches from them and have handed two of them over to N/P/ Pte Siabuta to soften and straighten out for me before proceeding further with them. Spent the evening reading and turned in at 9.30 p.m.

Sunday 1st April 1906

Big game shooting season opens. All Fool's Day. Tpr Watkins station duty. Received the following mail per the 9.10 train this morning: letter from father, p.p.c. from Cyril, also the *People* of March 4th date. *Practical Photographer Annual* for 1905; *Practical Photographer* No. 20 and No. 543 of *Hobbies* from Dawson & Sons.

Portingale walked up after the mail train had left about 10.30 a.m. and stayed to lunch. Dan pretty seedy; Dr Kennedy sent for and found in his usual place, half cut in the Railway Bar. Porty and myself strolled round the mine after lunch and I took some photos with a Brownie No. 2. After which we walked up to his room at the Loco Quarters and spent an hour or so looking at the papers he had got pictorial periodicals mostly and also had had some tea and fruit etc. After I bought some grapes and apples and strolled back to camp arriving in at 6 o'clock. Had

---

[75] Part of the Meikles Group—now one of Zimbabwe's largest retail and hospitality companies

the skoff dished up and made some soup for Dan and spent the evening reading etc till 10.30.

Monday 2nd April 1906

Rose at 8 o'clock this morning prepared breakfast, dismissed stable parade and had horses turned out to graze. Issued rations for Native Police and prisoners etc. Breakfast. Went round obtaining a list of white residents here this morning also obtained some wood from the coolie store, Kuper. Lunch. Spent the afternoon doing some carpentry. Issued horses' and donkeys' rations at 6 p.m.. Dismissed evening stable parade. Dinner. Spent the evening reading and filing home letters etc. Turned in at 11.30. Dan much better and out of bed today. Got my store bill from Meikle Bros etc today. Developed in machine a spool of the No. 2 Brownie films I exposed yesterday, all views of the Colliery screens etc.

Tuesday 3rd April 1906

An alteration takes place in the train service from today by which we gain a week on the English mails and in future get our letters Saturday mornings instead of Sundays.

I spent the morning doing odd jobs in compound, cleaning up generally etc. Lunch at 1.30. I spent the afternoon doing some carpentry started to make a chest of drawers and table combined etc. Later on I assisted Dan and Watkins to make and fit a new disselboom[76] to the Scotch cart. Dinner 7.30. Saw to the donkey horses etc. Dressed at 11 o'clock saw the S.C.[77] inspanned and went with it down to the station to meet the train and get Lieut Agar's kit etc. Arrived back in camp at 1.43 a.m. and immediately turned in. Lieut Agar arrived on tonight's mail [train].

Wednesday 4th April 1906

Mr Agar came up to camp last night and we fixed him up in Dan's room and put a bed in ours for Dan. We all rose at 6 o'clock this

---

[76] *Disselboom*: wagon shaft
[77] S.C.: Scotch cart

morning Marriott went down to the station with the S. cart to fetch Mr Agar's kit etc. I prepared breakfast took the stable parade issued rations etc. Dan made up his returns etc assisted by Atkins. Had breakfast at 8.30. After breakfast Marriott and myself got out the stores and equipment and checked it over etc ready for Mr Agar to take over.

Mr A has ordered a saddle, arms and kit inspection for 10 o'clock tomorrow morning. I spent the afternoon clipping out my kit and also a portion of the evening. Wrote two letters posted up my diary, had a smoke and turned in at 10.30 p.m. Sent Xmas number 1904 of *Argus Annual* to Sissie; photos of Soc's to Mother.

Thursday 5th April 1906

Stables 7.30. A coolie reported having died this morning of Blackwater fever, prisoners on fatigues cleaning up camp. Breakfast 8 o'clock. Prepared for inspection. Saddlery arms and kit inspection at 10 a.m. by Lieut Agar. I prepared lunch. Wrote a letter to McLocklin[78] and another to Sgt Tweedy.[79] Lunch 1 o'clock. Counted over and checked generally as to dates etc. 10oz received of L.E.[80] and rifle ammunition. I met the train from Vict. Falls at 2.51 and returned to camp at 4.30 and read until 5.30. Stables 5.30. I took the parade, issued rations etc. Spent the time till dinner at 7.30 yarning with Watkins.

Printed, developed and fixed etc 8 1/1 plate Bromide views of Wankie Colliery also 5 No. 2 Brownie Bromide views. Turned in at 11.30.

Friday 6th April 1906

Camp routine as usual today. I spent the day doing carpentry and cooking the meals. Also mounted 7 1/1 plate views of Wankie Colliery and sent them down to *Inceni* Woods for sale @ 3/- each. Dan went down below to the hotel to skoff with *Inceni* this evening. Watkins is in

---

[78] This may be 332 William George McLoghlin, who attested six months after Clarke and left time-expired on 23 July 1905.

[79] 301 Herbert John Tweedy, attested 21 June 1902

[80] Light explosive?

the office and I am reading and doing little odd jobs for myself. The mail train arrived shortly after midnight and with the English mail instead of Sunday at 9.10.

Saturday 7th April 1906

Mail train arrived at 1.30 a.m. this morning. Tpr Marriott met it on the station. Lieut Agar went to Vict Falls on the same train at 2.30 a.m. I spent this morning planing hippo hide and making it into walking sticks and sjamboks, riding whips etc.

I got the following by mail today when the post office opened: nothing. Mail didn't arrive. The De Luxe from Cape Town was late and consequently missed the connection with the Zambezi Express also the Zambezi Express broke down and had to leave a 3rd Class coach, the Dining Car and Caboose at Malindi and arrived here at 1.50 a.m. with only a 1st and 2nd Class coach and a Guard's van besides the engine and tender. The same train came back from the Falls at 5 o'clock this afternoon and proceeded into Bwayo at 5.30. I made a cement well in front of one of the water tanks this morning and after having lunch at 1.30 spent the afternoon planing hippo hide to convert into riding switches. Spent the evening writing letters and reading and turned in at 10.10 p.m.

The mails and 3rd Class passengers left at Malindi are supposed to arrive by special train at 1.57 a.m. tomorrow morning.

Sunday 8th April 1906

Dan and Watkins went for a ride before breakfast. I prepared breakfast. Marryatt lay in bed until we had started breakfast at 9 o'clock and then came to the conclusion that it was about up to him to get up if he wanted any breakfast. He arrived in the skoff hut just as we finished. A goods train arrived at 11 o'clock this morning but no mail (European) only the local mails. I went down to the Butchers after breakfast and ground two plane irons and then returned to camp and finished planing some hippo hide. Spent the afternoon reading. Made an apple pie for dinner tonight (which filled to exceeding fullness). Mr Giese arrived and pitched his camp just below our kopje. Mr G dined with us and we spent the evening yarning for a while on the verandah after this I posted up my diary wrote a letter read some articles in the *Amateur Photographer* and then turned in at 11.30.

Monday 9th April 1906

The ordinary passenger train arrived and brought with it the European mail at 12.30 a.m. this morning. Watkins met it. Marryatt took over cook for the week from me this morning. I got the following mail when the post office opened this morning: a Watson's Enlarger for use with a Pocket Kodak, they omitted to send the magnesium attachment ordered with it. Catalogue from Hughes re: alphinge enlargers, sample bromide enlargement from Raines & Co. Ealing and quotations re: enlarged negs etc; letter from David Allan, letter from Cyril enclosing P.P.C., also a P.P.C. from Sis; letter from Watson & Sons explaining why the magnesium attachment not sent etc. *Sunday Chronicle* from Cyril.

I spent the morning reading my mail etc. Made a hippo hide riding whip in the afternoon and with the exception of silver mounts finished it. Mr Giese strolled up in the evening and we yarned until bed time at 10.30.

Tuesday 10th April 1906

Prisoners on fatigue putting fresh *daga*[81] on the stable walls all day. Marryatt turned in at 10.30 a.m. with a dose of fever. I spent the morning reading and writing letters etc. In the afternoon I superintended the prisoners working. In the evening Dan, Watkins and I sat in the skoff hut and discussed horses, bits and bicycles until about 10.30. Read until 12.20 and then went down to meet the train from town. Two native police arrived with a couple of prisoners, there was a parcel from McLochlin for me containing 1 tin blacking, 1 tin saddle soap, sandpaper, emery paper, a tobacco pouch, 4 pairs 1 in. butts and

---

[81] Mud and cow-dung

screws, 1 tin of grey paint, 1 Swan No. 1 Fountain pen. There was also a parcel of books sent to us from Mr Carey R[esident] Magistrate Bwayo, who was up here recently holding court. Train was late and I got to bed at 2.30 a.m.

Wednesday 11th April 1906

This morning rose again at 6.30 and breakfast at 8 o'clock. Inspanned the Scotch cart and carted up manure for *daga* etc. Wrote to Cyril enclosing stamps and bromide brownie No. 2 views of Colliery. Wrote to McLochlin giving size of Pathe legging required also for 1½ oz of magnesium ribbon, magnesium attachment for A. R. enlarger, 6 pkts Imp. P. Ms Bromide paper. Read until lunch time at 1 o'clock. Went down to the station to see two N/P off to Bulawayo but found train would not leave until 8.05 p.m. so sent them back to camp. Spent a while in the P.O. yarning with "Porty", and then bought some pears from the Coolie greengrocer and returned to camp. Dan , and Giese out for a ride together. Dinner 7.30. I spent the evening writing my mail for the next post and turned in at 10.30 pretty tired only having had 4 hrs sleep last night. Sent two P.P.C.s to Sis, and wrote to mother and Cyril, returned photos to J. & W. Arnsley Esq Whittlesea.

Thursday 12th April 1906

Rose early this morning and walked about until breakfast at 7.30. Stables at 8 o'clock—prisoners on fatigue putting fresh *daga* on the floor and walls of the spare hut and mess hut. I spent a portion of the morning reading. Lunch 1 o'clock. I met the train from Vict. Falls at 2.51 p.m. Mr Fuller, A.N.C., passed through on his way to Bwayo, Fonseca left today for Balalema. Posted my mail. Noticed a very pretty and altogether dainty little damsel in the first class carriage in fact the most charming girl I have yet seen in Rhodesia, evidently from Home judging by her fresh clear face. On return to camp I painted my cleaning kit-box etc. Dinner 7.30. Spent the evening reading, turned in at 10.30 approximately.

The grazing guard lost the horses and they didn't arrive in camp until late this evening. Marryatt still sick in bed—fever. Fire occurred in Bwayo. Charred human remains found believed to be Tpr Pym[82] B.S.A.P.

Friday 13th April 1906

Usual camp routine. After breakfast I superintended prisoners working on the garden placing manure round tomatoes etc. Caught three horned beetles. Read till lunch time.

Paid off Chalela and discharged him. Pay 10/- 13 August till 13 Sept. £1 13 Sept till 13 Nov. £2.10.0 less 4/- from 13 Nov till 13 April/06. Lunch 1.30 p.m. spent the afternoon straightening up kit and filing old letters from England and doing odd jobs for myself. Spent the evening writing to Sis. Watkins meets mail train at 1.51 a.m. in the "wee small hours" of tomorrow morning.

Saturday 14th April 1906

8 o'clock went down for mail. Received *Photographic Apparatus Making and Repairing* from Watson & Sons Holborn. Letter from W. Taylor, Aston, Birmingham, stating goods ordered were being sent at once and giving information etc. Mail train left late and did not arrive until 4.00 a.m. this morning cause "hot box" on the engine.

Spent the morning doing odd jobs about the camp. Lunch 1.30.

Spent the afternoon manufacturing a riding whip from hippo hide— read various works on photography until dinner time at 7.30. Spent the evening reading and turned in at 9.30 for want of something better to do. Mr Giese left this evening and went back to Pandamitanga. The mail train passed through at 3.30 on the return trip to Cape Town from the Falls. She now does the trip from Cape to Zambezi in under 4 days a distance of 1572 miles, and the mails take 21 days to do the 7500-odd miles in.

---

82 Pym: actually Pim

Stamps   1/0

Sent Xmas number of *Argus*[83] *Annual* to Sissie

Sent photos to Mother of Rhodes' funeral and enlarged photos of Victoria Falls etc.

Sunday 15th April 1906

Until I turned to this page this morning I really wasn't aware that today is Easter Sunday. Anyway it is just the same in all respects to us here and having no parson or a church we get no service so one Sunday is very much like another, in fact unless we look at a calendar occasionally we aren't sure of the day, date, or anything else. I engaged a fresh savage named Jonas at 10/- per month this morning.

Mr Agar and Sgt Godfrey went to Bongela's Kraal at 7 o'clock this morning for some shooting and are expected back tonight. I wrote a long letter of 26 pages and an extract from Bulawayo *Chronicle* to Sissie enclosed some stamps which occupied me all the morning and about 20 mins after lunch—had a nap in the afternoon. Note received from the Doctor at 5.30, reporting that White the ganger at 273 Cottage has committed suicide, it may be he has been murdered by his boys. Watkins to investigate.

Monday 16th April 1906

Mr Campbell the new A.N.C. for Sebungwe arrived on last night's mail train at 1.15 a.m. Slept in camp in Dan's room also had breakfast with us this morning. Watkins gone out to the Deka on duty. Lieut Agar and Sgt Godfrey also gone to the Deka on duty. I packed a consignment of stores for Matese after breakfast, issued passes, wrote a letter to the Business Manager, W[ankie]. Colliery, read for a while.

Dan and Mr Agar returned from Deka at 12 o'clock and we immediately had lunch. I was down at the cemetery all the afternoon digging a grave for White with a gang of natives. White buried at

---

[83] *Cape Argus* newspaper

sunset. I duties did gravedigger and sexton all in one and remained and had the grave properly filled in and the earth baked over it. Returned to camp at 7.30 and had some dinner. Dan arrived back in camp about a quarter of an hour after me and we dined together. Tpr (Sausage) is sick and I have given him some medicine. I hope he isn't sickening for distemper, poor old chum. Read for a while and then turned in. Tpr Watkins arrived back from Deka with White's effects about 5.30 p.m.

Tuesday 17th April 1906

Dan left on patrol to Pandamatenga and the Bechuanaland Border with the Scotch cart today. I spent the day in bed with fever, temperature at midday 103.6. Gilgood[84] the new N.C. for Sebungwe arrived on tonight's train. Usual camp routine. Nothing of special note occurred.

Wednesday 18th April 1906

I spent the morning in bed, but having reduced my temperature to normal and feeling much better I got up about midday and lolled about camp all the rest of the day. Gilgood N.C. and Campbell A.N.C.[85] Sebungwe left for Tshete with 111 carriers this morning, and Gilgood's kit etc. I wrote a few postcards to Sis, Cyril, Mother, and Hilda also one to Arthur.[86]

Watkins and Lieut Agar went out to the Deka Pumping Station at 2 o'clock this afternoon on duty, connected with the suicide of White, a ganger of 273 Cottage.

Thursday 19th April 1906

I spent the whole day in bed having got up sooner than I should have done. Camp routine as usual; nothing unusual occurred. Pass[enger] train from Victoria Falls at 2.51 this afternoon.

---

[84] Valdemar Gielgud
[85] A.N.C.: Acting Native Commissioner
[86] Clarke's brother

Friday 20th April 1906

I got out of bed after breakfast this morning and spent the day reading. Watkins and Marryatt spent the afternoon down at the range fixing up the targets etc.

I had my first meal for 4 days this evening, having subsided on slops i.e. milk, Brand's Essence etc during the last few days. English mail arrives at 12.30 a.m. Nothing of note occurred today.

Saturday 21st April 1906

English mail day—incoming mail at 12.30 but outgoing mail closes at 5 and mail train leaves at 5.30. Mail as follows received this morning:

Sample from Taylor Birmingham, pens etc, invoice of goods despatched from Taylor Birmingham, catalogue from Watkins and Doncaster, Invoice from Wm Dawson and Sons, Publishers; letter from Lloyds, letter from Marconi & Co., letter from Father enclosing one from Mother, also letter and *Sunday Chronicle* from Cyril, No. 546 *Hobbies*.

Went down to the station to fetch up a consignment of goods. Posted my mail and returned to camp at one o'clock with Portingale who remained to skoff with us. I took a couple of photos in the afternoon and messed about with Porty in camp here. Spent the evening reading. Watkins and Marryatt went down to the store in the evening and returned some time after midnight. It has been trying to rain all the evening but didn't succeed. I heard today that the remains of Late Cpl Pim were interred with military rites during the last day or so.

Sunday 22nd April 1906

Lieut Agar and Tpr Watkins left for Jackies Kraal this morning with the intention of working the Deka River and vicinity to Deka Bridge for game and returning tomorrow morning. Marryatt and myself were working down at the butts from 10.30 till nearly 5 p.m. Volunteers trying to pass out for their trained course when they get the £8 grant for each efficient man. Porty came up from the Range with us and stayed for skoff with us, leaving shortly after. 15 natives deserted from Wankie Colliery today.

Train arrives from Bulawayo at 12.30 a.m. Far. Sgt[87] Smith expected to be on board, Marryatt has kindly consented to meet the train for me as I have contracted another infernal cold and it is raining pretty heavily. I turned in after sending down a Police Boy and prisoners for Smith's kit at 1 o'clock.

Monday 23rd April 1906

Public Holiday in Rhodesia today. Arose at 7.30, breakfast at 8 o'clock. Watkins and Mr Agar arrived back at lunch time. Prisoners employed cutting poles to make me a dark room. Watkins says they saw no game and only got a leopard and one pheasant between them. I met the train from Victoria Falls in the afternoon obtained a copy of the first issue Livingstone Pioneer. Spent the evening enlarging packet Kodak to ½ plate on bromide in Watson's enlarger and with magnesium ribbon. Turned in at 12.30 p.m. Nothing unusual occurred.

1 Pr Pathe Leggings, 1½ oz magnesium ribbon, 6 pkt imp., Platino matt rapid Bromide paper received from Cpl McLochlin this morning.

Tuesday 24th April 1906

Sgt Smith shod the horses this morning. I received a letter from Geo. Errington this morning enclosing 12/- M.O. for Postcards sent him. I spent the morning superintending prisoners erecting a hut for me to make a dark room of. I spent the afternoon making a fitting a door etc. I spent the evening making ½ plate enlargements from P.K. negatives 22 in all. Train arrived from Bulawayo at 12.30. Sgt Smith went Victoria Falls.

---

[87] Farrier Sergeant

Wednesday 25th April 1906

Arthur's birthday. Court sits here today on duty in court all the morning etc. Spent the afternoon cleaning kit etc. Spent the afternoon entering useful data and formulae in my book for that purpose. Wrote some letters. Turned in at 9.30. 7 prisoners paid their fines and went today. Nothing of special note occurred.

Thursday 26th April 1906

Sgt Godfrey arrived in from Patrol this morning. Court sat again this morning to hear two cases. I spent the morning cleaning my saddle and writing letters. Addressed two P.P.C.s to Sis Gaydon. Sgt Smith rearrived on this afternoon's train from Victoria Falls. Mr Agar's horse contracted horse sickness and stands a good chance of pegging out.

I spent the greater portion of the afternoon reading. Made two enlarged ½ p negatives and enlarged about 20 bromides during the evening.

I have given Sgt Smith authority to bid for Tpr Pym's photographic apparatus when it is put up for auction in Bulawayo and to buy it in if possible in its entirety, going up to £10 or £11 if necessary.

Friday 27th April 1906

I overslept this morning and did not wake until breakfast was on the table. Tpr Marryatt sick. *Livingstone Pioneer* No. 1 and some photos sent to Cyril. Photos sent to Sissie.

Mr Agar rode out to Deka River on duty. I spent the day doing various petty jobs in camp. In the afternoon went down to the P. Office. Enlarged some negs onto Bromide ½ Plate in the evening. Turned in at 11.30. Nothing unusual occurred.

5/6 enclosed in a letter to Pearl Camera Co.

Saturday 28th April 1906

I received the following mail at 10 o'clock this morning:

P.P.C. from Sissie saying she will write to me by the next mail. I am a bit disappointed having been looking forward to a letter for the last fortnight. However I can live in hopes of a letter next mail now. Letter from Mother stating Arthur won a prize for History. *Hobbies*, letter from Tylars Birmingham.

Lieut Agar held an Arms Inspection at 10.15 of us and the Native Police. Usual camp routine for the rest of the day. Lieut Agar's horse still sick, but now expected to pull through. Sgt Smith left on the afternoon train for Bulawayo.

Sunday 29th April 1906

Sunday routine. Watkins and myself spent from 10 till 1 and again from 2.30 till 5.25 marking down at the range. Sgt Godfrey in Bed. Fever Marryatt lying down, fever, slight attack.

Lieut Agar out shooting, bag nix ni. He rode Bobbie. I met the train from Bulawayo at ½ after midnight (12.30) 2 N/P arrived from Bulawayo one of who was from Salisbury duty escorting a prisoner from Salisbury to Tshete Sebungwe District, via Bulawayo by rail to Wankie and by road to Sebungwe distance about 400 odd miles, not bad carting a prisoner that distance. Returned to camp and went to bed at 1.30 a.m.

Monday 30th April 1906

I laid in till just before breakfast this morning. Breakfast 8.30. Spent till 11.30 having a bit of a spring cleaning in my portion of the room. Served a summons on Walter Gibbon, blacksmith on the mine, for assault on a native. Returned to camp. Prepared dinner. Met the train from Vict. Falls at 2.51 a.m.

A. A. J. Werner was on the train bound for London (used to be manager of Copthalls Stores Geelong when I was stationed there). Obtained tickets for and saw on the train 30 of our native police bound for Bulawayo. Spent ½ an hour in the P.O. had a cup of tea with Porty. Returned to camp. Took stable parade, issued rations, prepared dinner and then read till dinner time. Spent the evening reading and posting up this diary from last Friday till tonight—am now going to bed at 10.15.

Tuesday 1st May 1906

Rose early this morning and pottered about till 7 o'clock and prepared breakfast. Took stables, issued rations. Breakfast 8 o'clock etc. I spent the morning writing in the Office. Lunch at 1.30 p.m. Spent the afternoon mixing chemicals, overhauling my camera and labelling bottles and boxes etc. Wrote up some notes in my formulae book in the evening and turned in at 11.30. Usual camp routine. Nothing of note occurred.

Wednesday 2nd May 1906

Watkins met the train from Bulawayo at 2.15 this morning. I rose and prepared breakfast. Repaired the football and patched the case, also soled a pair of boots. Served up lunch at 1.30 p.m. Spent the afternoon cleaning kit.

We had a game of soccer from 5.30 till 6.30 this evening. Marryatt and Watkins went down to the Store to see Lear. I spent the evening reading. Dan , went to bed at 8.30 p.m. I did later at 9.30.

Thursday 3rd May 1906

Marryatt went down to the station to consign some stores to Malesi. I rose at 7 and made some curry for breakfast. Watkins, Dan , and I had a kick about with the footer till breakfast time it being a nice cool morning. After breakfast I cleaned some kit. Served two subpoenas on whites at the mine. Borrowed a footer pump from Cobs and then returned to camp prepared lunch. Blew up the football. Lunch 1pm. Letter received from Smith, Bulawayo; Cpl McLochlin with my bill for good amounting to £3.1.3 enclosed.

Friday 4th May 1906

Mr Agar, Tpr Watkins, 2 native Police and their own private servants with 4 pack donkeys left camp this morning on a 3 weeks patrol in the vicinity of the Gwaai River.

I got a slight dose of fever and lay down after taking my temperature (102.4) and some quinine etc at 11 o'clock a.m. Mr Farrer, N.C.[88] arrived in camp from Tshete in the Sebungwe District bringing with him about 40 natives, carriers etc. Sgt Godfrey left for Matise on tonight's train to prosecute in case Rex v Walter Gibbon, assault. I had some soup and more quinine this evening and feel much better. Temperatures at 6.30 (99.4) Turned in at 9 o'clock after posting up my diary.

Saturday 5th May 1906

I feel alright again today and got up and prepared breakfast. Spent from ten o'clock till 5 minutes to three writing to Sissie in reply to her letter P.P.C. to her also, one to Cyril. Dan rearrived from Matise on this afternoon's train.

Mail received the long looked for letter from Sissie, paper from Cyril, *Hobbies*. Nothing of note occurred this afternoon. Mr Farrer came up to camp at 5 o'clock and obtained various papers, issued passes to his Native Messengers. Marryatt and Dan did not come up for dinner but stayed down at the station. I went to bed at 6.30 and had a cup of tea and had some medicine; feeling seedy again.

Sunday 6th May 1906

I got up for breakfast and had some porridge. Spent the whole day lying on my bed, no food midday some soup in the evening. April pay arrived from Bulawayo. Everything very quiet here, nothing of note occurring today.

---

[88] N.C.: Native Commissioner

Monday 7th May 1906

I spent the whole day lying down, still having the fever. Camp routine as usual. A poor beggar on the wallaby[89] arrived in camp this afternoon with the usual pitiful yarn, no food, no work etc. We gave him a bed up here and dinner tonight and breakfast tomorrow and wired the C. C.[90] Bulawayo for further instruction re him, and pauper assistance, etc.

I got up in the evening being much better and made some rawhide boot-laces from a duiker skin. Also cut out and tanned a pair of knee strappings for my riding breeks. I spent a portion of the evening reading and turned in at 9 o'clock after taking some mutie.[91] Train from Vict Falls passed through at 2.57. Sir W. F. Hely-Hutchinson and Lady Hutchinson were on the train returning from a visit to Vict Falls with several officers, orderlies etc.

Tuesday 8th May 1906

We have a poor beggar on the wallaby in camp here. It seems he has had a bit of a rough time of it and is a bit light-headed. Nothing worth mentioning happened in Wankie this day. I spent the morning printing postcards for Marryatt and toned them this afternoon, also mounted a 1/1 P Photo for Marryatt. The evening I spent letter writing.

It seems the fellow who got natives from here on Sunday had also had a bad time of it he told Marryatt he was lost for 6 months in the bush in Belgian territory. Full moon rose at 5.57 here this evening. I should have met the train from Bulawayo just after midnight. It arrived at 2.51. Just about when I was getting ready to go down to the station a note came up from Dan who was down there to say not to come down as he would remain and meet the train. He slept down in *Incemi* Woods' room.

---

[89] "On the wallaby track" = Australian slang meaning itinerant and seeking work
[90] C.C.: Civil Commissioner
[91] From Zulu/Ndebele *uMuthi*: medicine

Wednesday 9th May 1906

Marryatt arrived back in camp about a quarter to four this morning and woke me up to give me a bit of news etc. We yarned till dawn, he then went to bed about an hour later. I got up inspanned the animals in the Scotch Cart and with Dan proceeded down to the station to fetch up stores comprising mealie meal, mealies and trusses of hay. This occupied me until 1.30 when we had lunch. In the afternoon Dan and I stacked the hay and got the grain and meal into the store and locked it there.

In the evening I wrote to Sissie and posted up the diary and turned in early, "dead beat", and slept like a top till dawn.

Thursday 10th May 1906

Got up about 7 o'clock this morning and pottered about till breakfast time at 8 o'clock. Stables till 9. Spent the morning writing letters etc and I think Marryatt and Dan did the same.

Nothing of note occurred camp routine as usual. I did some copying from 12 x 10 photos later on in the morning. Had a nap for want of something better to do in the afternoon and spent the evening reading.

Friday 11th May 1906

Marryatt went down with the cart to fetch up stores, broke the disselboom first trip up from the station. The prisoners and police boys carried the stores from off it into camp and we pushed the cart up between us. After breakfast we amused ourselves till lunchtime putting in a new *disselboom* after having made the same.

In the afternoon I had a sleep and later made a pie and jam tart for dinner tonight. I wrote a letter, read and boxed up kit till one o'clock a.m. and then went down to meet the train at 1.51 a.m. from town. Box of chemicals and photographic equipment from Bwayo canteen, cost £3.13.0. I got back from camp and turned in at 2.30 a.m.

Saturday 12th May 1906

Marryatt and Dan went down to the station before breakfast. I rose at 8 o'clock and after dressing etc unpacked and checked off goods received last night. Spent the morning after breakfast reading my mail which consisted of letter from Father, P.P.C. from Sissie, *Practical & Pictorial Photographer, Studio Series* No 1 from Dawson & Sons and invoice and letter from McLochlin after this I spent the morning fitting a new shutter release to my camera and mixing chemicals and later issued 8 natives with passports to leave the Territory.

Lunch at 1.30. After lunch I went round the mine and took the following photos: 1 1/1/ plate view of the Wankie colliery new screens, result very good; 2 ditto result a trifle thin; 3 ½ P view of Mine, result fair but thin; 4 view of the Loco quarter and engines etc, result very good. Returned to camp and sensitised some cards of writing paper. Sgt Godfrey went to Bulawayo with prisoner Nashu and escort of 1 N/P.

Marryatt went to meet the train and remained down there. I dined in solitary state in consequence. I spent the evening developing plates and sensitising rough papers for printing on tomorrow. Read for a while whilst papers were drying and then went to bed. I finished my letter to Sissie. Wrote to Father and also to McLochlin, returning invoice as requested today.

Sunday 13th May 1906

Rose at 8 o'clock, prepared breakfast. Spent the morning printing and toning postcards and 1/1/ P prints etc, addressed 2 P.P.C.s and photos to Sissie.

After lunch I took my camera and went round the mine taking photos. I took 1 1/1 P of the mine general view from Kopje, 1 1/1 P of screens etc looking S.S.W. and 3 ½ P views from off the screens. Returning I took a group ½ P of four of the fellows on the mine, also exposed 8 Brownie films on views of the mine. I spent the evening with the Orderly and in Tom Roame's room looking at his negatives and photos. I had skoff with them at the mine boarding house. Returned to camp about 12 o'clock and went to bed.

Monday 14th May 1906

Rose up prepared breakfast at 7.30 this morning. Marryatt went down to the station to fetch up goods etc. I remained in camp; issued a few passes to natives. Printed and toned some P.P.C.s and ½ P prints also proofs of the negs taken on Saturday. Lunch at 1.30. I spent the afternoon reading, Marriott met train from Vict. Falls. Mr Fuller the A.N.C. arrived from Matise. A special train with people from Jo'burg passed through here at 2.30 this afternoon, the train was made up of C.S.A.R.[92] rolling stock.

In the evening I developed the plates of films exposed yesterday, result all splendid negatives, some of the best I have yet turned out. Read till 12.30 whilst plates were drying and then went to bed.

Tuesday 15th May 1906

Camp routine as usual. Nothing of note occurred during the day. I spent the morning printing and toning to pass the time and execute some orders etc. In the afternoon I issued some passes and read until stables at 5 o'clock—issued rations, took stable parade, prepared dinner. After dinner I printed and developed some gaslight papers till 10 o'clock. Marryatt went down to the station and sent up for the stretcher and as many boys as possible at 12.30. Dan arrived back from Bwayo bringing with him the man Dalton (the wallaby who was here a few days ago). He had attempted suicide and had been found in the Veldt near Mabindi by natives.

Wednesday 16th May 1906

Paid Jonas 10/- today, 15/4/06 to 15/5/06.

---

92 Central South African Railways, successor to the Imperial Military Railways of South Africa.

After breakfast this morning I went down to the hospital to relieve Creedon the hospital orderly, and took his place to watch and look after the man Dalton as soon as the Dr had sewn his throat up. It appears he cut his throat about 3 days ago with a pen-knife and very nearly finished himself, in fact we could see the back of the tongue, but he had missed the jugular. The Dr says if the wound does not fester he will pull through in short, if it heals in from three weeks to a month he will be alright but if not it will not heal and he will die. If he pulls through he will in all probability go to Pretoria asylum, being a bit mad.

Marryatt relieved me at 2.30 and I came home and lay down till the evening feeling seedy. I read for about an hour in the evening and then turned in and passed a pretty bad night, awake till four in the morning.

Thursday 17th May 1906

Except that I feel as if a mule had kicked me in the small of the back, I am alright today and got up and prepared skoff. I shall take Dalton to Bwayo as soon as he can be shifted, and see the Doctor in camp there myself, also take my rifle in and get the broken pull-through taken out by Sgt Wickwar[93] the armourer. Marryatt released Creedon down at the hospital until after dinner and then I went down and relieved Marryatt till the evening, when Creedon came on again for the night.

I came home after skoff and read for about half an hour and then got to bed and took 10 grains of quinine.

Friday 18th May 1906

I got up and prepared breakfast. Marryatt sick, malaria. I relieved Creedon at 9.30. The R.C. Priest arrived from Bwayo to see the sick man and had breakfast and lunch in camp. I returned to camp at 10 o'clock and had to fly round and prepare skoff for our guest. I had a sleep in the afternoon and in the evening went down to the hospital and sat the night out with Dalton. He seems to be getting a bit more insane every day, and if he wasn't so weak would probably be dangerous. I had

---

[93] 302 Francis Thomas Wickwar, attested 6 July 1902.

to watch continually last night for fear he should tamper with the bandages on his throat.

Saturday 19th May 1906

I woke Creedon at 6 o'clock this morning and came back to camp when he was ready to look after Dalton and immediately went to bed, getting up again at 10 o'clock feeling as if I had had no sleep at all.

I got my mail at 10.30. Letter from Sissie, letter from Vera Offer and one from Cyril also parcel of photographic goods from Tylar, Birmingham.

I spent the remainder of the morning issuing passes to natives and after lunch had another sleep after having addressed P.P.C.s to Sissie and Winnie Gaydon also Mrs Offer, Mother and Cyril.

Dan went down below for skoff this evening and I took stables issued rations etc. After dinner I wrote for a while and then went down to the hospital again for the night.

Sunday 20th May 1906

I put in the morning at the hospital. Lieut Agar and Tpr Watkins arrived from Patrol this morning at 12.30 a.m. and brought some Birds with them.

I had a sleep during the afternoon and after dinner in the evening went up to the hospital to look after Dalton till 1.30 when Creedon relieved me and I came home and to bed. Nothing of note occurred today, usual Sunday routine.

I heard from Watkins that Mrs Scott from at N'gamo is dead and also that the Blakewells have lost their youngest child, 1 ½ yrs old, recently.

Monday 21st May 1906

I spent the morning doing odd jobs in the camp. Watkins went to the hospital to relieve Creedon till dinner time. I spent the afternoon studying a Kodak manual.

Marryatt met the train at 2.51 from Vict. Falls. After stables in the evening we had a kick at the football. I wrote to Mrs Offer and started a letter to Sissie in the evening. Nothing of note occurred.

Tuesday 22nd May 1906

Breakfast 8.30. I spent the morning cleaning kit and doing odd jobs in camp. In the afternoon I went to the station and Post Office and spent about an hour with the P.M. in his office. Marryatt left with the Scotch cart and donkeys to do the Pandamatenga patrol, at 4.30 this afternoon.

Mr Giese came up this evening and he and Dan went down to the hotel later. Watkins and myself had a kick at the football for an hour or so after evening stables and after dinner (at 7.30) Watkins and myself passed the evening till 12 o'clock asking one another questions in Zulu and from a Zulu dictionary.

Watkins met the train from Bulawayo at 1.30 a.m. Train an hour late.

Wednesday 23rd May 1906

Lieut Agar left for Vict. Falls on last night's train. I went down to the hospital to relieve Creedon for a few hours.

Thursday 24th May 1906

Victoria Day, Public Holiday in Rhodesia. Watkins and myself went into Bulawayo in charge of James Dalton on this afternoon's train. He was very quiet and gave us no trouble. We dressed his throat for him twice during the trip. Upon arrival in town at 8 o'clock a.m. Friday, we found Sgt Ferminger[94] with an ambulance waiting for us and from the station proceeded to the Jail and handed Dalton over to the Head Warder and then we stopped on our way back to the camp and had a B & S[95] all round after which proceeded to camp and arrived in time for

---

[94] 5 Ronald Firminger, attested 10th October 1896.
[95] B & S: brandy and soda

breakfast. I went into Hospital[96] and Watkins returned to Wankie at 1.30 this afternoon. The S.R.V. Sports are on today and most of the fellows from Bulawayo camp attended. Being in "dock", I did not go. In the afternoon I strolled over to the canteen with "Pills" and had a few soft drinks, and spent the evening talking to some of the fellows in camp till 12.30, when I turned in.

Friday 25th May 1906

Saturday 26th May 1906

I remained in the Hospital all day and was successfully treated by 11 o'clock tonight. I shall have to have a couple of days to pick up and then can return to Wankie. I spent the whole day reading and the evening also.

Saturday 26th May 1906

See Friday 25th and read for today.

I have entered the last two days up together on Thursday's page.

Sunday 27th May 1906

I spent the morning in the Hospital reading and the afternoon playing billiards and looking through the week's periodicals and newspapers.

In the evening I went to church and after Church Sangster,[97] Davies,[98] Fubbs,[99] Greathead,[100] Ginn and myself went up to the Drill Hall to listen to the band of the S.R.V.s, which plays every Sunday evening from 9 till 10.30. We had a cup of tea and some Wads[101] at Walker's stalls and at half time interval I met several fellows I knew belonging to

---

[96] Nowhere in his diary or service records does Clarke describe the reason for his trip to hospital.

[97] 436 Charles Reginald Sangster, attested 27 December 1902.

[98] This is probably 703 Glyn Louis Davies.

[99] 235 Samuel George Fubbs, attested 31 October 1901.

[100] 761 Wilson Greathead, attested 26 January 1906.

[101] Sandwiches.

the B.A.C.[102] and Raylton F.C.s[103] and altogether passed a pleasant evening after the band I returned with the others to camp and went to bed.

Monday 28th May 1906

I was discharged at 9.30 this morning cured from Hospital and went over to the office; got an advance from Capt. Tomlinson[104] and put in a pass to visit town for the day. I went out of camp at 2.30 and after buying a few articles of kit I required at MacCullough and Bothwells I visited a few friends and dined with Sid Sinden at 6.30. We then went round to the 'Palace' to see a couple of Sinden's chums and about 9.30 I left them and called in for a drink at the 'Empire' on my way home and met Hooten,[105] one of the old chums from Gwanda and stayed there talking with him whilst we were talking in walked Ginn, Fubbs and Alexander (who was in from Gwanda).[106] We stayed there playing snooker till closing time at 12.30. Ginn, Fubbs and I then adjourned to the Avenue Café and had some supper after which we returned to camp and to bed.

Tuesday 29th May 1906

6 recruits arrived in camp this morning and proceeded to Salisbury at 9.30. They are all from the S. A. Constabulary. I returned to Wankie today leaving town at 10.30 on the station I met Jock Fair,[107] one of our fellows who was going to Kalomo[108] as a duty Sgt in the B.N.P.[109] and

---

[102] Probably Bulawayo Athletics Club.

[103] Raylton Football Club. Raylton is a suburb of Bulawayo with a large and long-established Sports Club and cricket ground.

[104] Later Colonel, retiring with the rank of Acting Commissioner.

[105] 154 Frederick Hooten, attested 12 June 1901.

[106] 383 John Alexander, attested 5 September 1902.

[107] 397 Charles Henry Fair, who attested on 1 October 1902. Fair completed two years in the B.S.A.P and re-enlisted six months later as 656 Charles Henry Fair on 17 March 1905; he was appointed to the the Barotse Native Police on 28 May 1906 and by 1916 he held the rank of Lieutenant-Colonel.

[108] In present-day Zambia.

[109] Barotse Native Police.

we shared a compartment as far as Wankie. After dinner we adjourned to the dining car for "Wets" and a fellow traveller gave us some music on his gramophone till 11.30. I arrived in Wankie at 12.40 and after bidding Jock goodbye I proceeded up to camp and went to bed.

Wednesday 30th May 1906

Passed a very quiet day overhauling kit in camp. Got the following mail: letter from Mother, one from Cyril and a P.P.C. from Sissie also the *Practical Photographer* for April from Dawsons. Camp routine as per usual.

Thursday 31st May 1906

I rose at 7.30 and prepared breakfast—stables 8 till 8.30. Breakfast at 8.30. After breakfast I wrote a letter and repaired a pair of boots and some saddlery. Prepared lunch.

Tpr Marryatt arrived back from the Pandamatenga patrol at 2.30 this afternoon. Tpr Watkins met the train from Vict Falls at 2.51. I spent a portion of the afternoon reading and later prepared dinner. C. M. Hamilton sent us up 2 Guinea Fowls, a Sequshle[110] and two Namaqua Partridges.[111]

We spent the evening spinning yarns in the rooms till 11.30, when we went to bed.

Friday 1st June 1906

Rose and prepared breakfast. After breakfast I spent the morning cleaning my saddlery and at 1.30 we had lunch. I spent the afternoon cleaning my rifle and equipment. Watkins and Marryatt did the same. I stuffed and cooked the birds for tonight's dinner and took evening stables. Dan Godfrey, Watkins and Marryatt went down to the Hotel and I remained in camp and wrote letters for tomorrow's mail. I met the mail train from Bulawayo at 1.51 a.m.

---

[110] A francolin, Zulu = isikwehle
[111] Probably sand-grouse.

Saturday 2nd June 1906

Lieut Agar held a saddle and arms inspection at 10 o'clock this morning and afterwards inspected the Native Police. I received 2 P.P.C.s from Sissie and another from J. Annesley, Whittlesea, acknowledging photos by today's mail. I have been busy doing odd jobs in camp today in expectation of Major Straker[112] the C.S.O. for Matabeleland arriving to inspect stations shortly.

Nothing of a special note occurred today. I met the train from the Falls at 5.15 p.m. no-one in particular on board. Sent a p.p.c. to Sissie and a letter to Cyril by today's mail. I spent the evening reading till 10.30 and then went to bed.

Sunday 3rd June 1906

A very quiet day in camp. I have had a bit of the Blues all day and have almost decided to apply for a transfer back to Bwayo at the end of the month, failing my being transferred to the Falls. I spent the day trying to read.

In the evening after dinner I went down to see McMurbey at the mine and after that went on to the store to see Lear and Porty and returned with Marryatt at 11.15 and to bed. Marryatt met the train from Town at 12.30 a.m.

Monday 4th June 1906

I went down with the S. Cart to the station to consign a quantity of stores to Crosthwaite[113] at Matese. The *disselboom*[114] broke and the boys had to *pajamesa*[115] the stores to the station after breakfast I overhauled kit etc. and spent the remainder of the morning reading. In the afternoon issued passes to natives, took evening stables, issued rations

---

[112] Straker had joined the British South Africa Company's Police—the forerunner of the B.S.A.P.—in 1890, just too late to join the Pioneer Column which annexed Rhodesia.

[113] 622 Herbert Maitland Crosthwaite, attested 21 June 1906.

[114] Waggon yoke

[115] Phakamisa = pick up/carry (Zulu)

etc for Dan Godfrey. Spent the evening reading and writing to Sissie. Marryatt and Watkins have gone down to the store and Dan to bed feeling seedy. I am now going to bed, time 11.35 p.m.

South Bucks Free Press received from Cyril this morning with an account of the R. B. Hussars[116] camp at Wycombe.[117]

Tuesday 5th June 1906

Camp routine as usual. Nothing occurred at all usual. Humdrum and routine today.

Wednesday 6th June 1906

Trains from Bwayo and Falls passed through here today. Watkins met them. I spent the day mending the Footer and reading. Also issued passes to natives and cooked the meals.

Thursday 7th June 1906

Nothing of note occurred today.

Friday 8th June 1906

Mr Fuller A.N.C. held court here today. I spent the day making a pair of cupboard doors for the mess hut etc. and the evening writing to Sissie.

Saturday 9th June 1906

Mail day. Letters received from Sissie also P.P.C. and letter from Mother. I spent the morning finishing cupboard doors. I wrote to Sissie or rather finished my letter this afternoon. I met the train De Luxe from Vict Falls at 5.15. Tprs Davidson[118] and Waters[119] on board proceeding

---

[116] Royal Buckinghamshire Hussars: Clarke's Yeomanry regiment. Following service in France in the First World War, he obtained a commission in 1916 in the Royal Bucks Hussars.

[117] High Wycombe, Buckinghamshire.

[118] 438 William Wallace Davidson, attested 2 January 1903 and deserted on 3 February 1907.

[119] 157 Thomas William Waters, attested 18 June 1901.

to Bwayo. Davidson on leave to England and Waters to Town on duty. I spent the evening reading and posting up my diary.

Lieut Agar and Sgt Godfrey have gone to Merrimans Kraal for a weekend's shooting and will be back Monday morning next. Yrs truly in charge as Senior Trooper in the meantime.

Sunday 10th June 1906

I spent this morning reading and the afternoon I assisted Watkins to repair his shotgun and showed him how to take the parts to pieces. Later I made a "Treacle Duff",[120] guaranteed to kill on sight.

The evening I spent reading and posting up my diary. Marryatt and Watkins have gone down to the store. At 12.30 Marryatt met the train from Bwayo. Tpr Davis, the Reg. tailor arrived and remains here to alter kit etc.

Monday 11th June 1906

I spent the morning repairing a pair of boots and reading.

In the afternoon Davis and myself went down to the mine for Davis to have a look round and from there we went down to the Hotel and remained to dinner at 7.30. After dinner we returned to camp and after reading for a while went to bed.

Tuesday 12th June 1906

I amused myself this morning putting new buttons on the football and writing up this diary for the last few days. In the afternoon I made some pastry, a cake (I said cake) and a Bread and Butter Pudding for tonight's skoff. At 5.30 we all turned out for a game of footer till sunset.

After dinner in the evening, Marryatt, Watkins, Davis and myself played bridge till 12.30, when we went to bed. Tpr Davis altered some of my kit for me this morning. Farrier Sgt Smith passed through on tonight's train and will be back here on Saturday next to shoe horses.

---

[120] Steamed treacle pudding.

Wednesday 13th June 1906

I took the stable parade for Dan this morning whilst he drilled the Native Police which he has been doing now for the past ten days at 7 till 8.30 in the morning and from 4 till 5 each afternoon. After breakfast I repaired a boot and cleaned kit till lunch time. In the afternoon I slept till 4.30 and then turned out for footer till dark.

I am cook this week from Sunday last. In the evening Marryatt went down to the store and later Dan and Watkins went down below to raid the Loco compound for prisoners. Davies and myself remained in camp reading till about 10.30 when we turned in.

Thursday 14th June 1906

Spent the morning painting a cupboard for the mess Hut and cooking the meals for the day. The rest of the day I spent issuing passes and reading. In the evening we played bridge, Watkins being my partner; we did very well, winning a rubber in two hands with no trumps on three occasions.

Paid Jonas 10/- this afternoon from the 15/5/06 to 15/6/06.

Friday 15th June 1906

Nothing occurred today. I wrote a few letters and P.P.C.s and killed time as best I could for the remnainder of the day.

Saturday 16th June 1906

I received a letter from Mother and a P.P.C. from Sissie by today's mail. Nothing of note occurred.

I spent the afternoon printing photos for Davis.

Tpr Marryatt left for Matese to take the clerk to the A.N.C. from Tpr Crosthwaite by the mail train yesterday or rather at 1.51 this morning. Sgt Godfrey accompanied him and returned on the afternoon train. Myself on station duty.

Sunday 17th June 1906

Lieut Agar and Tpr Watkins left on Patrol to Pandamitanga district for ten days, taking the Scotch cart and donkeys with them.

Monday 18th June 1906

Nothing of note occurred. Camp routine as usual. I spent the day repairing kit, sewing on buttons etc, and in the evening read till 9.30, when I went to bed. Tpr Crosthwaite passed through here on his way for Bwayo and his discharge being time exed;[121] from there he goes to Canada.[122]

Tuesday 19th June 1906

Stables and breakfast as usual. The prisoners are clearing the square of stones. I got another dose of fever and went to bed. Tpr Davis left for Victoria Falls on tonight's train. I got up in the evening and did the station duty at 12.30, seeing Davis off; the train was 45 mins late.

Wednesday 20th June 1906

I spent the day working in the office and copying photos in my spare time. In the morning I developed 4 plates and a spool of films.

Dan got a dose of shakes and went to bed at 10 a.m. and remained there for the rest of the day. I dined in solitary state in consequence.

Thursday 21st June 1906

I spent the morning printing photos and reading and cleaning kit. In the afternoon I met the train from Vict Falls at 2.51 p.m. Dan Godfrey still sick in bed but much better today. I dined in solitary state again today and am doing the In Charge business during Dan's sickness. Sgts Armfield and Scott[123] passed through here on their way to Bwayo by

---

[121] Time expired, i.e. come to the end of his period of service and decided not to re-enlist.

[122] Could Crosthwaite's example have helped to encourage Clarke to settle in Canada?

[123] Two possible Scotts in the B.S.A.P. at this time. With the rank of Sergeant, this may well be 72 Arthur Edgar Scott, attested 1 October 1898.

this afternoon's train. From what I gathered the Falls is as quiet as Wankie at present. This evening I spent reading and letter writing for the English mail.

Friday 22nd June 1906

The winter season commenced in Rhodesia today and continues till the middle of September. I spent the day issuing passes, writing letters and reading. Also cooking the meals in the evening. I mended some kit. The train de Luxe, English Mail etc arrived at 1.51 a.m.

Saturday 23rd June 1906

I received by the English Mail this morning 3 P.P.C.s from Sissie, also a letter, and from Cyril two newspapers. After breakfast I served a summons on Burns, one of the miners, for assaulting a native, and on my return wrote a letter to Sissie also one to Clarke at the Falls, at 4.30 p.m. I went down to the station to meet the train for Bwayo from Victoria Falls. The grazing guard boy reports that he has seen the fresh spoor of a lion at the back of the Range facing our camp and about ½ a mile away. Says the spoor is a big one, probably an old lion too old to hunt his food. The evening I spent reading till 10.30, when I turned in.

Sunday 24th June 1906

Breakfast at 9 o'clock usual Sunday routine. Cpl Henry Ford passed through by train this moirning. Two mules arrived for this station also Mr G's dog; I went down to the station and detrained them. The afternoon I spent reading till 4.30 and then I took Bobbie and the dogs out for exercise.

The evening I spent reading and at 12.20 I met the Falls train from Town, Sgts Armfield and Scott on board. I took over a prisoner from Armfield and returned to camp.

Monday 25th June 1906

Breakfast at 8.30. I spent the morning working and later toned some prints. In the afternoon I altered and repaired two pairs of Buller leggings and then met the train from Vict Falls. S J.P. A.N.C. Fuller.

Tuesday 26th June 1906

Nothing of note occurred camp routine as usual.

Wednesday 27th June 1906

Court sat here today. We were all busy with cases etc. Nothing of importance happened.

Thursday 28th June 1906

I spent the day cleaning kit, preparing saddlery and equipment for patrol. Nothing of note occurred. A very quiet day in camp, routine as usual. I met the train from Bulawayo at 1.51 a.m.

Saturday 30th June 1906

Rose at sunrise this morning. Packed two donkeys and started them away to Merriman's Kraal with instructions to wait for me at Bongela's Kraal. They were in charge of N/P Dubane and I also sent Dick and Jonas, my boys, with him.

I remained behind in camp to breakfast and to get my mail. I received a letter from Father and two P.P.C.s from Sis, also a Chesham paper with the account of Mr Fourmy's[124] funeral in. These I put in my haversack and proceeded to saddle up the mule (K12) I was taking with me. She objected and we had a bit of trouble to get the saddle on then proceeded to mount and got one foot in the stirrup but she bucked and I could not get into the saddle, so Dan held her and I had another try and succeeded after this. She had to be chased away from camp and it took

---

124 Fourmy was a solicitor practising in Chesham High Street as a partner in the firm of Albin Hunt and Fourmy.

over 4 ½ hours to get to Bongela's Kraal, a distance of 9 miles from here. I got her along by making her buck and run most of the way.

After offsaddling for a while on the riverbank at Bongela's Kraal I put the packs off the donkeys onto the mule and walked myself, from here I proceed about 9 miles to the Big tree outspan near Merriman's old kraal. I arrived here just about dark and offsaddled for the night. I built fires to keep any undesirable visitors away and then proceeded to feed the animals and myself afterwards. Dined off cookies, coffee and hare, read by moonlight for a while and then went to sleep.

Sunday 1st July 1906

Rose at sunrise this morning; saw the mule and donkeys fed, had a cup of coffee. Saddled up the mule and donkeys and proceeded over the hills to Merrriman's Kraal where we arrived at midday, the path being a tortuous one in and out of spruits, through mealie lands and over boulder strewn kopjes by native footpath. Whilst passing through the mealie lands I shot a brace of guinea fowl and several pheasants.

At Merriman's we offsaddled for midday halt to graze and water the animals and get some food and a rest ourselves. Here I took a couple of photos, one of a portion of the Kraal and one of the place where I outspanned. From here we went on to Jacobs Kraal, about seven miles further, where we offsaddled for the night; fed and watered the animals and then had our own meals. I dined off guinea fowl and after talking with the natives for a while went to sleep.

Monday 2nd July 1906

We have a long trek in front of us today, so I had the animals fed before dawn and exactly at sunrise we left Jacobs and proceeded on our way to Dingaans Kraal, 30 miles distant. Shortly after leaving Jacobs and whilst walking ahead of the remainder of the patrol I saw a duiker and as my own gun was somewhat out of order I shot it with the Police Boy's Martini Henry rifle put a bullet in the chest and right through the body and out at the near side flank, when the remainder of the patrol came along I had it strapped on the top of one of the pack donkeys and we proceeded from here the trek was uneventful until we reached Big Fley where there was plenty of water, so we offsaddled (it being about 11 o'clock) for a few hours to graze the cattle, get some breakfast and to skin and dress the duiker. After this was done we saddled up again and proceeded on to Dingaan's Kraal where we arrived about half an hour before sunset and just See slip [the continuation sheet has been lost]

Tuesday 3rd July

I was discharged by order of a Board of R.A.M.C. Officers under Para 18 05 XVI *King's Regulations* Authority Nos. D.D. of 24th/6/01 on this date 1901.[125]

I arose at dawn this morning and after feeding the animals and having a cup of coffee we proceeded on our way across Dingaan's mealie lands and into the Gwaai Forest through which we travelled for an hour or more. We then arrived at the Dett River and crossing this we passed through the mealie lands belonging to some Bushmen (Chief's name Jackalossi) and camped on the rise above the lands for a short halt till after midday, here I shot several guinea fowls and a brace of pheasants. After grazing the cattle we had some Breakfast and then as stated I did a bit of shooting after which we saddled up and proceeded to what is known as the topside of the Dett, travelling through more forest and arriving at a small Kraal the chief of which is known as Jonas. Here we halted for the night.

[On continuation sheet slipped into the diary] 3 Tuesday continued. We arrived at Jonas's Kraal about 3.30 in the afternoon and stayed there as I had contracted a dose of malaria and did not feel up to continuing further on. The natives here were very good and when Dabane the Native Police boy I had with me said I was sick they made a bed of grass

---

[125] This entry relates to Clarke's earlier service with the 21st Lancers regiment, which he joined in October 1900 and with which regiment he served for less than a year before being discharged as no longer physically fit for service. It is curious that less than four months after being discharged from the British Army as unfit, Clarke had joined the British South Africa Police

and leaves for me to lie on and built up a couple of good fires for me, also fetched me milk and eggs. I got into the blankets and had a cup of hot coffee and 15 grains of quinine and after tossing about a bit went to sleep and woke up on the following morning feeling quite fit again.

Wednesday 4th July 1906

Feeling alright again this morning I decided to proceed so after feeding the animals and I had had a cup of coffee and the sun had rise we left Jonas's Kraal and proceed to Dickerts Farm and the Gwaai river. The first part of the way was through forest and big timber and from this we came out onto the uplands above the Gwaai river covered with shorder, dense bush and long grass, and then onto more Kaffir lands passing through these and leaving Dickerts Farm about a mile on our left we continued our journey as far as Chatham's Farm on the bottom end of the Skikuma Fley just where the fley becomes a small river and about three miles above its junction with the Gwaai River. Upon arrival we found that Hawthorne who had charge of the farm for Chatham was gone into Malindi for stores and would not be back for a couple of days. We offsaddled here for a few hours and I had some buck and also made bread, we grazed the donkeys and had a

[On continuation sheet slipped into the diary]

Rest and then saddling up the donkeys again proceeded back along the bottom road as far as Dickerts Farm where we turned up from the river and passing Dickerts Homestead it being after dark went to Dalalungungu's Kraal just at the back of the Homestead where we offsaddled for the night and after feeding the animals and getting some food ourselves turned in and went to sleep.

Thursday 5th July 1906

As I had plenty of time I did not trek this morning but turned the animals to graze and then went down to see Dickert and stopped there yarning for about half an hour after which I took some photos in the Kraal and then put in the rest of the morning reading. About 2.30 we saddled up and proceeding back by the same route passed Jonas's Kraal also Jackalassis and camped at a small kralal on the north side of the Dett for the night. Here after feeding the animals as usual I had some dinner and shortly afterwards changed the plates in my dark slides for moonlight, and after this read for a while by moonblight. The moon was being at the full or nearly, I then went to sleep.

Friday 6th July 1906

I had the animals fed at sunrise and before starting we had our own breakfast. We then saddled up and proceeded to Dingaan's Kraal the trek being back over the same track as the forward journey through the forest and an uneventful one except that the donkey packs came off twice and caused delay. We arrived at Dingaan's about 11 o'clock and stayed till about 3.30 p.m. We then saddled up again and proceeded on our way after leaving the kraal and saw a duiker and got 5 shots at it out of the Lee Metford (Gov. rifle I have) and missed every one. I then gave it to the Boy I had with me in disgust and took the shot gun from him and stalked the duiker and got him with both barrels at about 15 paces after about 20 minutes stalking. I returned and placed him one of the pack donkeys and we proceeded on our way to Big Fley arriving about 8.30 p.m. and off saddled for the night. I fed the animals and built the fires etc whilst Dubane and my boys cleaned, skinned and dressed the duiker. I dined off liver, shortly after turned in.

Saturday 7th July 1906

The animals were fed about an hour before dawn this morning and at dawn we moved off again trekking to Jacob's Kraal and offsaddling at the water under the shade of some trees. During the trek I had a long shot at a running steinbuck but missed but later on got amongst some guinea fowl and got 6 of them in about 5 minutes, four shot on the run and the other two with a parting shot from each barrel as they rose in the air. Also about two miles from Jacob's kraal I shot 3 pheasants.

We remained at Jacob's during the midday heat and grazed the animals etc. I made some fresh cookies and had some lunch and breakfast in one and then went to look for pheasants in the mealie lands—I got a pair. About 3.30 we saddled up again and went to Merriman's Kraal arriving just after sunset. Here we remained the night and Merriman brought me some M'Bude-Bude and eggs and the boys some mealie pap. After having something to eat I talked with Merriman for a while and then went to sleep.

Before leaving Merriman's the following morning I took some photos.

Sunday 8th July 1906

We left Merriman's at sunrise and as the boys wanted to go round by the transport road to Big Tree outspan instead of over the Hills we went and found that instead of about 9 miles over the hills we had nearly as much climbing and descending to do and that the road took us round about 19½ miles, we arrived at Big Tree about 2.30pm, very tired and disgusted and not having seen so much as a "go away" bird[126] during the trip in the shape of anything living. At Big Tree we offsaddled for two hours and after having some food I took the shotgun and went to look for game. The first thing I saw was a hare which I bowled out, and after that I got 5 pheasants in quick succession and returned to the outspan quite satisfied. From here we proceeded to a small kraal on the Incesi river and stayed the night, and as we had run out of meal I got the women to crush some mealie into meal for us. About 9.30 I turned in.

Monday 9th July 1906

We saddled up about an hour after sunrise after we had had some breakfast and I had taken some photos and proceeded round the river Incusi to Sichutae's Kraal where we stayed for about an hour and had some M'Budi-Budi. We then proceeded straight into camp along the Tshete road and arrived at about 3 o'clock, en route I shot 3 pheasants. I landed in camp with 3 pheasants, 1 duikah and a hare, and the boys with 2 rock rabbits I had shot for them. Upon arrival I found that Lieut Agar, Sgt Godfrey and Watkins were in camp, and that Watkins was in

---

126 The grey loerie, whose call sounds like "G'way".

bed with his head bound up having had an argument with a mule and been kicked in the right eye, and that he had 5 stitches put in by the Dr, 3 in the upper and two in the lower eye lid.

I got cleaned up generally and read my mail and passed the rest of the day quietly in camp. Letters received from Father, Cyril, Mother and two PPCs and letter from Sissie for which much thanks. I was glad to get them after ten days absence.

Tuesday 10th July 1906

I spent the day in court, Fuller the J.P. being here to hold court we had several cases up for hearing.

In the evening I developed the photos I had taken on patrol and in each instance the exposure development etc were alright but in a few instances the natives had moved during exposure and spoilt the plates, at 12.30 I met the train from Bulawayo and got to bed at 1.15am.

Wednesday 11th July 1906

Paid Jonas 15/- today and sacked him having engaged a better savage in his place about ten days ago. At 2.51 I met the train from the Falls and spent the evening reading and printing photos on bromide paper. Camp routine as usual today, nothing of note occurred.

Thursday 12th July 1906

I spent the day cooking the meals and lunging the mule that had stretched out Watkins. The evening I spent reading and turned in early. Camp routine as usual, nothing occurred to break the monotony.

Friday 13th July 1906

Lunged the mule again today.

Had a bit of fun with the mule, it took four of us 3 hours 50 minutes to put a pack saddle on him in the morning and in the afternoon we tried to get a pack on him and succeeded but he broke the saddle, a wooden one, and bucked clean through the debris and getting away from the boys cleared into the bush. We got him back about a quarter of an hour before dark and gave him about half an hours lunging and I think about as rough a time as he ever had in his life, anyway he was completely tamed when we put him in the stable. The evening I spent posting my diary up to date and writing letters.

Saturday 14th July 1906

Mail day. 2 PPCs from Sissie, nothing else. Lunged the mule in the morning. Wrote to Sissie sent photos in albums to mother and Sissie also PPCs to Sissie and Cyril all of which missed the mail thanks to the stupidity of my new savage at 5 o'clock I met the train from the Falls and in the evening wrote two letters and a portion of one and did odd jobs for myself till 11.30 when I went to bed.

Sunday 15th July 1906

Having nothing better to do Dan and I lunged the mule and as he objected to being saddled and tried to kick us etc we just lassoed his hind legs from under him and threw him, saddled him and put a good 200lb pack consisting of dirt in sacks on him and then lunged him until he was so tired he laid down completely done. I think a few more doings like this will take some of the vice out of him; it is pure vice, he kicks and bites if he gets the opportunity, needless to say he hadn't a kick or bite in him when we had finished. I don't know if he is very sore, but my shoulders ache from manipulating the long waggon whip we had to keep him running round with.

The afternoon, I spent sleeping and later had a hot bath, the first I have had in the country (first hot one, I mean). The evening I spent reading and later met the train from Bulawayo at 12.30am.

Monday 16th July 1906

Camp routine as usual today. I lunged the mule in the morning, repaired a pair of boots and met the train from Vict. Falls in the afternoon. Mr Giese arrived in from his farm at midday and later walked up here and stayed a while. The evening I spent reading, Watkins did the same, and Dan rode out with Giese to the waggons at 9.30. We went to bed.

Tuesday 17th July 1906

I spent a portion of the morning printing from some negatives Portingale lent me a day or two, ago in the afternoon I lunged the mule and after reading for about 20 minutes in the evening after dinner I went to bed for want of something better to do.

Camp routine as usual, nothing worthy of recording occurred.

Wednesday 18th July 1906

I spent the morning doing odd jobs about the camp. Watkins served a summons on Santos the butcher, N/P Dubane left for N'Gumu with a led horse to hand over to the patrol from Bwayo. I went down to the station in the afternoon to make a few enquiries (officially). Later I toned some prints and spent the evening reading.

Thursday 19th July 1906

Sgt Godfrey left on today's train for Bwayo on duty. Watkins met the train from Vict. Falls at 2.51, this afternoon a native arrived from Victoria Falls and was sent into hospital here with a broken leg.

I did odd jobs about the camp and spent the evening reading. Watkins spent the evening down at the store.

Friday 20th July 1906

Watkins and myself only in camp today.

After breakfast Watkins went down to the station to fetch up a consignment of stores. I received a photo postcard from Sissie which had kindly been sent to Umtali first and should have arrived last Saturday. The morning I spent in the office.

In the afternoon I rode out to 273 cottage to see the Ganger re some natives and got back at 5.30, he made the mess a present of some cockerels. The evening I spent writing letters and posting up this diary.

A native woman died in the railway compound this afternoon. Prisoners arriving in from Likete this morning, deserters from the colliery.

Saturday 20th July 1906

Lieut. Agar left for Victoria Falls on last night's train at 12.20 (Sunday night).[127] I was busy repairing a portion of the stables during the morning and later superintended the native police and prisoners cleaning up camp. In the afternoon I met the train from Vict. Falls. Lent my Kodak to *Incemi* Woods to take to the Falls.

I was taken sick again (more fever) after returning from the station and went to bed and had a bad night, being sick several times during the night. Letters from Cyril and Mother and two PPCs from Sissie by today's mail.

Sunday 22nd July 1906

Watkins as well as myself sick today and everyone else being away we put in a very unpleasant day between us two, both being in bed for the major portion of the day. Lieut. Agar left for Vict. Falls on tonight's train not yesterday. We got up and made a pretence of having dinner in the evening but shortly went back to bed.

Another bad night for both of us. Camp routine as usual for Sundays i.e. morning and evening stables only duties for the day.

Monday 23rd July 1906

We got up today both of us feeling a trifle better and roamed about in camp doing little odd jobs. I wrote some letters in the afternoon. Nothing of note occurred today. Camp routine as per usual.

---

[127] This entry is marked *Sunday not today.*

Tuesday 24th July 1906

Nothing worthy of note occurred during the day. I issued a few passes and for want of something else to do read most of the day.

At 12.30am I met the train from town. Sgt Godfrey returned on it from town. The administrator's private coach was also on the train he being on his way to the Falls and N.W. Rhodesia.

Wednesday 25th July 1906

The morning I cleaned kit. The afternoon I wrote a letter and read till 5 o'clock and then took "stables". The evening I spent reading.

Dan and Watkins went down to the Hotel after dinner this evening. Nothing of note occurred today, except that one of the fellows on the mine had all his kit stolen from his room whilst he was on shift. Sgt Godfrey came back from Bulawayo at 12.30am. I met him at the station.

Thursday 26th July 1906

I was on station duty this afternoon. Farrier Sgt Smith arrived by goods train this evening having missed the passenger train. Lieut Agar came back from his visit to the Falls this afternoon.

I amused myself during the evening making camera bags for use on patrol.

Friday 27th July 1906

I assisted Sgt Smith this morning when he shod the animals. Later attended to the meals for the day.

In the afternoon I wrote some letters to Sissie, Cyril and Mother also PPCs to Sissie and Cyril, photo to Sissie.

The evening I spend reading. Watkins met the train de luxe from Bulawayo at 1.51am. Capt Tomlinson was on board and proceeded to Vict Falls to inspect that station.

Saturday 28th July 1906

Sgt Godfrey left on patrol this morning to Kazengula and the Bechuanaland border taking with him 3 donkeys and the Scotch cart also pack saddles as he intends sending the S cart back from Mr Giese's from Pandamatenga and proceeding from there with pack donkeys, he also took 3 native police with him.

N/P Pte Simwarara went to Limalanga's Kraal (Limalanga Chief Induna of District) and returned this evening reporting Limalanga very sick.

I went on patrol to Licasi[128] Station taking N/P Pte Sondusa with me. I returned from there re-arriving in camp at 8.30pm with 2 native prisoners. I shot a plover going there but did not get another opportunity to shoot anything after that. The evening I spend reading the *People* and the *Bucks Herald*. Letter from Sissie by today's mail.

Sunday 29th July 1906

I sent N/P Pte Indebele in charge of two native carriers to Tshete with the hut tax tokens today. I went down to the Hospital to see Creedon in the evening. In the afternoon I cleaned my saddlery and equipment for inspection tomorrow morning.

Portingale and Morris came up to camp and stayed a while this morning and we helio'd to Dan who was posted with another Helio on Dumichesa.

Monday 30th July 1906

Saddlery, arms, equipment and camp inspection this morning by Capt S_____[129] O/C 'K' Troop[130] who expressed himself as very well pleased with the state of the camp and our turnout generally.

---

128 Lukozi
129 Name indecipherable
130 K Troop was the BSAP Troop that covered Bulawayo magisterial district, which included Wankie.

I was informed by Capt. S that I shall be sent to Vict. Falls, relieve Tpr Davidson as soon as men arrive from Salisbury to make up the strength of this troop. After this inspection I had to march N/P Pte Londuza in front of Tommy[131] who fined him 2/6 for drunk at Livingstone recently whilst on patrol there.

I met the train from Vict Falls in the afternoon and in the evening posted up this diary and [illegible], turning in at 10.30pm.

Tuesday 31st July 1906

I went to Locusi on patrol today leaving camp after breakfast and returning on the following morning. Four native police arrived from Bulawayo and two from Matesi. Watkins and ten native police arrived. Leave on Friday for duty in the Sebungwe district during the collection of Hut Taxes.

Wednesday 1st August 1906

I returned from Locusi Station about 10.30 this morning having completed my business there and stayed the night. Had some breakfast on return and then did a bit of work in the office.

The afternoon I spent reading and doing the cooking etc. At 5 o' clock I took the stable parade and issued rations. We had four native police arrive here from Bulawayo on tonight's train for a special patrol in the Sebungwe district.

Thursday 2nd August 1906

Tpr Waters arrived here from Vict Falls for duty vice Watkins who goes on a 6-week patrol in the Sebungwe district on the 4th in charge of native police. His Honour the Administrator was also on the train en route for Bulawayo. I spent the whole day in the office helping with the weekly returns for the O/C.

---

[131] Probably Capt. Tomlinson.

Camp routine as per usual. The evening I spent down at the hospital chatting with Fred Creedon till 11.30 when I came home and went to bed.

Friday 3rd August 1906

Waters met the mail train from town at 1.57am this morning. Watkins, one horse and 10 native police left camp this morning to proceed through the Sebungwe district on patrol. Our pay arrived from Bulawayo by mail train.

Saturday 4th August 1906

I received a PPC from Sis this morning by the mail. Nothing of special interest occurred today. Camp routine as usual.

Sunday 5th August 1906

Camp routine as usual. I spent the day printing photos and toning them. Letter received from Sissie at 10.30 this morning.

Monday 6th August 1906

I was on station duty today. N/P Sonduga rearrived from Bulawayo where he had been as escort for two lepers. We got another prisoner from the colliery today, one who had been on before for several petty offences. I wrote to George Errington at Umtali. Letter received from Hilda and Mother at 11 o'clock this morning. Hilda acknowledges receipt of paints.

Tuesday 7th August 1906

Medical Staff Sgt Scott arrived here from Vict Falls by goods train this morning and was reattested by the O/C and is on leave from tomorrow morning. He intends trekking up to the Lakes for his holidays and having a 6 months shooting trip.

N/P Magula returned with the Scotch cart and four donkeys from Mr Giese's farm Pandamatenga at 7.30 this morning.

Camp routine as usual. I have been working in the office all day and met the train tonight. Scott went down with me.

Wednesday 8th August 1906

Tpr 'Willie' Baker arrived this morning with a couple of prisoners from Bulawayo and returned this afternoon; from him I learnt what is happening in town. I have been employed in the office all day again today and look like continuing to do so until Dan Godfrey arrives as the O/C seems lost without assistance. The evening Waters and I spent yarning and turned in early.

Thursday 9th August 1906

I was on station duty at 2.57 this afternoon, Tpr Bain[132] went through to to Bulawayo escorting a white prisoner and also to attain his discharge, being time expired. I packed up and sent to Marryatt at Matire his month's rations for himself and native police this morning.

The new stores arrived for us from Bulawayo and were ridden upon the S cart from the station by Waters this afternoon. After returning from the station I made up the books in the office to date and then issued rations and took the stable parade etc. The evening I spent writing letters and posting up this diary.

Wrote to Conliffe Russell and Co., Paris[133] tonight to be posted on the 11th March advising them of T.M.O.[134] despatched.

Friday 10th August 1906

Lieut Agar inspected camp and equipment this morning at 10 o'clock. Wrote a long letter by instalments during the week to Sissie and

---

[132] 639 John Malcolm Bain, who had attested two years earlier

[133] Cunliffe Russell & Co were a financial firm based in Paris; while they had originally been stockbrokers, they also acted as a European agent for various lottery schemes that were illegal in the United Kingdom. Clarke was probably sending money for entry into a lottery or sweepstake.

[134] Telegraph Money Order.

finished it with the exception of answering any letter if one arrived by tomorrow's mail.

Saturday 11th August 1906

I spent the whole day working in the office. Received a letter from Sissie by today's mail. Nothing of special note occurred.

Sunday 12th August 1906

I marked for a prize shoot down at the range today. The st[ation] master won first prize: 10 guineas and Mr Kearney the General Manager of the colliery put up an excellent lunch for us all. In the evening we went down to the Hotel for a game of bridge. Returned to camp at 12 o'clock and to bed.

Monday 13th August 1906

Tpr Waters left for Matise on the train at 1am this morning to escort the Hut Tax money to Bulawayo, the amount being £1,057. Marryatt from Matise also formed part of the escort. Tpr McLoghlin arrived from Bulawayo for duty here by the same train, and not knowing where the camp was he 'outspanned' alongside the line until daylight and arrived at our camp at 7.15am.

This afternoon the 'sports' of Wankie indulged in a cricket match. The doctor picked up against Mr Stevenson the Business Manager; I was on Dr Kennedy's side and we lost despite my taking five wickets for nine runs.

Tuesday 14th August 1906

Camp routine as usual. I spent the day in the office and the evening reading.

Wednesday 15th August 1906

Nothing of note occurred today.

Thursday 16th August 1906

Wire from town saying I am to go to Victoria Falls by the next train on transfer. I started packing my kit in the evening.

Friday 17th August 1906

Handed over to Trpr McLoghlin this morning and finished packing my kit. McLoghlin rode out to Locuse on duty and did not return today. Waters went to 273 Cottage on duty and left me alone in camp for lunch at midday.

Saturday 18th August 1906

I left Wankie at 1.57 or rather should have done if the train had run on time; as it was I left at quarter to five this morning on transfer to Victoria Falls and arrived at the Falls at 9.45, the train being 2½ hours late.

I spent the remainder of the day getting fixed up in my fresh quarters and in the evening we had a fire made just off the square and sat round it (Davidson, Ford and myself) exchanging news and drinking hot toddy. At 11 o'clock went to bed.

Sunday 19th August 1906

Spent the day down at the Falls and took some photos etc.

Monday 20th August 1906

Camp routine as usual. I wrote some letters, a lady at the Hotel lost some articles of jewellery, Ford and myself went down to investigate but had no luck. Went up to the range in the afternoon with Mrs and Mr P.M. Clark and Davidson to shoot and made an average of outers at all ranges, very poor indeed. Spent the evening reading.

Tuesday 21st August 1906

A train arrived from Bwayo at 7am this morning, 2 passengers only arrived by it. Nothing of note occurred.

Wednesday 22nd August 1906

Davidson and myself had a walk down to the Falls this morning. Nothing of note occurred.

Thursday 23rd August 1906

At 10.30am I saw the train out and spent the remainder of the morning and the afternoon printing photos. The evening I spent reading and went to bed early.

Friday 24th August 1906

I spent the morning making a table.

A Colonel Manifold[135] of the Royal Artillery was in camp this morning.

The afternoon I spent reading and strolled down to the Hotel later. In the evening I wrote letters for tomorrow's post. A detachment of the Bechuanaland Protectorate Police arrived here from Lake Nagami[136] and put up in camp here; two officers, the assistant commissioner and some NCOs also some native police.

Saturday 25th August 1906

I went down to the station at 2.15 to meet the train de luxe from Bulawayo but found upon enquiry that it was 6 hours late so returned to camp and met it later at 8.20am. There was a fair number of people arrived and several ladies.

---

135 This can only have been Lieutenant-Colonel John Forster Manifold of the Royal Artillery.
136 Lake Ngami

I posted letters to Geo. Harding, Cyril, Mother, Hilda and Sissie, also to Ginn and McDowell[137] in Bulawayo.

After breakfast I toned some prints and then saw the train out for Bulawayo at 12.30, after which Ford and myself walked down to the Hotel and had a whisky and soda each and then returned to camp for lunch. The afternoon I spent glazing the prints I toned this morning and posting up arrears in my diary. The evening I developed 5 plates, views of the Falls taken on Wednesday last.

Sunday 26th August 1906

I met some visitors on my way down to the Falls this morning and stayed chatting with them instead of taking the photos I intended to. In consequence I returned to camp for lunch and after lunch I went down to the Falls taking my savage with me to carry the camera etc. I first proceeded halfway down the Gorge just below the Hotel and exposed a plate on the Gorge and Bridge; from here I went onto the Bridge and took a photo of the Falls as seen from there, and after this took four more photos of the Falls. The evening I developed them. The result, one very good one of the main Falls, the remainder all under-exposed owing to using slow plates, three of the six useless.

Monday 27th August 1906

A train arrived from town at 7 o'clock this morning, Davidson met it. The mail brought me nothing at all this week. The party of the Bechuanaland Police who accompanied the Administrator from Palapye Road up here left this morning on their return by train.

Nothing of note otherwise occurred today. I spent the morning doing odd jobs in camp the afternoon printing photos and the evening writing and reading.

---

[137] 534 Rowland McDowell

Tuesday 28th August 1906

Wrote to *Incemi* Woods re: No. 3 Brownie Kodak for sale etc, also to Moore Livingstone, promised to go over to Livingstone to take photos on Sunday next. Two native police returned here from the Sebungwe patrol, so evidently Watkins is back in Wankie.

Wednesday 29th August 1906

I met the train from Bulawayo at 3am this morning. By the mail I got a PPC from Sissie (also a spool of films from Dr Kennedy for development). Sent plates to W. Waters, Wankie. Superintended natives digging holes in camp for planting of trees etc. Wrote to Dr Adam Jameson at Pretoria re: a billet etc.

Thursday 30th August 1906

Trpr Davidson left on leave today for England via the Cape.

Monday 3rd September 1906

Received my English mail by this morning's train.

Tuesday 4th September 1906

Nothing unusual occurred. Usual camp routine etc.

Wednesday 5th September 1906

Tpr Waters returned here from Wankie by this morning's train and Tpr Thompson[138] arrived here also on transfer from Bulawayo; he is a newly joined recruit from Salisbury. Waters, Ford and myself went down to the Hotel this evening and from there to see the Falls by moonlight.

Friday 7th September 1906

I spent this afternoon on the river in a canoe.

---

[138] 792 Edward Clifford Thompson, who had attested less than five months earlier on 30 May 1906.

Sunday 9th September 1906

Waters and Ford went to Livingstone today, nothing unusual occurred.

Tuesday 11th September 1906

We all spent the day preparing for tomorrow's inspection.

Cpl Ford was sick this morning and I issued passes and did the office work for him. There was a dance at the Hotel in the Dining Hall this evening amongst the visitors and residents.

Wednesday 12th September 1906

Occupation Day (Mashonaland) Public Holiday in Rhodesia.

Lieut Agar together with Lieut Dacomb,[139] the Atg Ordinance Officer, arrived here from Wankie and inspected the station this morning. Native Comissioner Fuller J.P. arrived also from Matise and held court here, seven convictions, five fines paid and two natives doing h[ard] labour here.

I got my English mail: 2 papers and a letter from Sissie.

Thursday 13th September 1906

Tpr Thompson saw the train out at 9.45am, Lieuts Agar and Dacomb left by it. Lieut Agar to return to Wankie and Lieut Dacomb to B'wayo.

Ford went down to the Hotel and arrested three native deserters. I spent the morning writing, and went down to the river fishing in the afternoon. In the evening I wrote letters for the English mail.

Friday 14th September 1906

Settled Mess a/c with Wankie by a money order for £2.11.0.

Planted some vegetable seeds this afternoon, wrote PPC to B., S., W. and D. Gaydon, CC to C, ARC and Mother, letter to Sissie. Issued

---

[139] 17 Leonard Sydney Dacomb, who had enlisted in 1896 and retired with the rank of Lieutenant-Colonel

permits for blacks of cattle and saw the station master re: the same. Went down to the Hotel this evening and played billiards.

Saturday 15th September 1906

A Mrs Turnbull and the two Miss Turnbulls, wife and daughters of the late Judge Turnbull of Natal.[140]

This evening I spent down at the Hotel playing billiards.

Sunday 16th September 1906

Sunday routine. Nothing of note occurred.

Monday 17th September 1906

There were very few passengers this morning and nothing of note occurred during the day except that Cpl Ford and Tpr Waters left on a 14-day patrol to Kazangulu and left myself in charge of camp here, with Thompson for duty.

Tuesday 18th September 1906

Townend from the Hotel brought the Miss Turnbulls up about 10 o'clock to see the camp and they caught us nicely having breakfast. I showed them my photos and gave them some together with some mahogany beans.[141]

They remained in camp till 12.30 sitting under the office verandah chatting with Thompson and myself and this evening they and Mrs Brown sang songs and played to us in the music room at the Hotel, when I was introduced to Mrs Turnbull their mother; they are all very nice people and have invited me to visit them on my way home.

---

[140] Judge J.W. Turnbull of Pietermaritzburg, who died in about 1902
[141] The Natal Mahogany (*Trichilia emetica*) has brightly-coloured orange-red and black seeds

Wednesday 19th September 1906

Sgt Smith arrived on this morning's train and after breakfast he and I walked down to the landing stage and through the rain forest. Ginn and a party of friends also arrived, I dined with them at midday.

After dinner I received an invitation from the Miss Turnbulls to accompany them on the river to Livingstone Island and did so, we had a very enjoyable trip and I took several photos for them of various subjects; we rode to the landing stage there and back on mules, it was good fun and finally we landed back at 7.30, and after dinner the Misses Turnbull and Mrs Brown and some of the people living here sang songs in the Music Room at the Hotel till 10.30 when we wished the ladies good night.

Thursday 20th September 1906

The Misses Turnbull and their mother left on this morning's train as also did Colonel Chester-Master[142] and his sisters. In fact, there was a general exodus and there is not now a single visitor at the Hotel.

I am sorry the Miss Turnbulls left as they were very nice people, in fact the nicest I have met since coming to Africa.

Memo: Address, 204 Loop Street, Pitermaritzburg, Natal.

Invited to visit them there on my way home.

Friday 21st February 1906

Letters written to Dr Adam Jameson, Captains Cazalet[143] and Shawner and to Cyril, mother and Sissie. It is raining today for the first time this season, a nice steady fine rain which will do a lot of good and incidentally fetch out the mosquitos.

---

[142] Florence and Margaret Master.

[143] As a Lieutenant in the Mashonaland Mounted Police, Alexander P. L. Cazalet (1855-1928) had participated in the Jameson Raid, and subsequently became a Sub-Inspector in the Matableland Division of the BSAP.

Saturday 22nd September 1906

No visitors at all at the Hotel; everything very slack here, nothing of note occurred.

Sunday 23rd September 1906

Sinclair the Postmaster and myself visited the Falls and took some photos, developing them in the Hotel dark room in the afternoon. I dined with Mr Holland at the Hotel in the evening.

Monday 24th September 1906

The season Spring commenced today in Rhodesia and continues till Dec 22nd next. Cpl Ford and Tpr Waters arrived back from Kazengula this pm.

Tuesday 25th September 1906

Mother's birthday.

Saturday 29th September 1906

Pioneer Sergeant-Major Shettle[144] with Trprs Bloomer,[145] Carter,[146] Chard[147] and Shout[148] arrived in the morning train to erect a new gaol for natives and whites here. Nothing unusual occurred.

Sunday 30th September 1906

I accompanied some of the Pioneer staff to the Falls this afternoon.

---

[144] 59 Frederick George Shettle
[145] 696 Edward Parker Bloomer
[146] 704 John Purdon Carter
[147] 719 Harry Oswald Chard
[148] 803 Alfred John Shout

Monday 1st October 1906

Sgt Godfrey from Wankie, Tpr Marryatt from Matise and Tprs Lloyd,[149] Gooyer,[150] Pritchard[151] and Henchley[152] arrived from Bulawayo on special duty connected with the visit of H.E. Lord Selborne.[153]

Tuesday 9th October 1906

Parade for tomorrow rehearsed and kit cleaned during the day.

Wednesday 10th October 1906

H.E. Lord Selborne arrived this PM by special train and proceeded over to Salmon siding a mile over the other side of the river, thus saving a lot of guards etc. for us.

Thursday 4th October 1906

H.E. Lord Selborne left this PM. Lieut Agar, Sgt Godfrey and Trprs Gooyer, Lloyd, Henchley and Clarke[154] on special escort duty.

Friday 5th October 1906

A general holiday

Saturday 6th October 1906

Sgt Godfrey, Tprs Marryat, Lloyd, Gooyer, Henchley and Pritchard left on the morning train for their respective stations. Lewanika[155] also passed through from Seku on the train to interview Lord Selborne. Mr J. Broderick and Miss Broderick also left.

---

[149] 680 Francis Oswald Lloyd

[150] 478 Edward Bertram Gooyer

[151] 759 Samuel Frederick Pritchard

[152] 481 Douglas Percy Henchley

[153] Lord Selborne (1859-1942) succeeded Lord Milner as High Commissioner for South Africa and Governor of the Transvaal and Orange River Colony in 1905.

[154] This is probably 1155 Clark rather than Clarke himself.

[155] Lewanika (1842-1916), traditional leader of the Lozi nation of Barotseland

Sunday 7th October 1906

Ford, Shettle, Bloomer and self went to Livingstone for the day.

Monday 8th October 1906

My birthday, the 23rd one.

Had a large bottle of fizz just to mark the occasion at the Hotel this evening.

Wednesday 10th October 1906

Father's birthday. Also Ford's.

Bloomer and self went along the bottom of the gorge to the bridge this afternoon, the journey taking us 2 hours and 20 minutes constant climbing. I took some photos.

Thursday 11th October 1906

This afternoon Shettle, Ford, Waters, Thompson, Bloomer, Shout, Carter and myself accompanied by P.M. Clark went to the Falls and P.M. took our photo with the Falls for a background.

[This is the last regular entry in the diary, although there are a number of entries that Clarke clearly made earlier in the year:]

Wednesday 24th October 1906

Cyril becomes of age today.

Sunday 4th November 1906

Occupation Day (Matabeleland). Public Holiday throughout Rhodesia.

Thursday 8th November 1906

I complete 5 years' service with the B.S.A. Police today having joined in Cape Town on November the 8th 1901. They have been I think five of the pleasantest years of my life and if I have other years as pleasant in the future I shall not have much to grumble at.

Friday 9th November

Public Holiday for King's Birthday throughout Rhodesia.

Tuesday 13th November 1906

I joined the 21st Lancers on this date 1900 and was sent to Marlborough Barracks, Dublin, to be stationed.

Tuesday 4th December 1906

Shangani Day – Public Holiday throughout Rhodesia

Saturday 22nd December 1906

The summer season commences in Rhodesia today and continues till about the 22nd of March next.

BIBLIOGRAPHY

Gibbs, P. and Phillips, H., *The History of the British South Africa Police: 1889-1980* (Johannesburg: Covos Day, 2000);

Holland, H., *The Rhodesia Civil List 1902* (London: Jeppestown Press, 2011);

Lloyd, Jessie M., *Rhodesia's Pioneer Women* (Bulawayo: Rhodesia Pioneers' and Early Settlers' Society, 1974);

Maclean, J., *The Guardians: a story of Rhodesia's outposts, and of the men and women who served in them* (Salisbury: Books of Rhodesia, 1974);

Percy Fitzpatrick Institute of African Ornithology, *Roberts VII Names Database*, http://www.fitzpatrick.uct.ac.za/sites/default/files/image_tool/images/2 75/Publications/Roberts_VII_Project/Names_Database/Zulu.pdf

Sampson, R., *The man with a toothbrush in his hat: the story and times of George Copp Westbeech in Central Africa* (Lusaka: Multimedia Publications, 1972);

Wall, D., *Intaf's Men*, http://www.freewebs.com/dudleywall/ intafsmen.htm;

Wills, W.H., *The Anglo-African Who's Who and Biographical Sketchbook 1907* (London: Jeppestown Press, 2006).

INDEX

A

B

C

D

E

F

G

T

Tedder, Joseph, 21
Thompson, Edward, 81, 82, 83, 87
Tomlinson, Alfred, 11, 54, 72
Turnbull, Mrs, 83, 84
Tweedy, Herbert, 33

W

Waters, Thomas, 27, 57, 58, 74, 75, 76, 77, 78, 81, 82, 83, 85, 87
Watkins, Jesse, 5, 11, 13, 20, 21, 23, 25, 26, 28, 29, 31, 32, 33, 34, 35, 37, 38, 39, 40, 41, 43, 44, 45, 51, 52, 53, 55, 57, 58, 59, 60, 67, 68, 70, 71, 72, 74, 75, 81
Watson, carpenter at Wankie mine, 24, 25, 37
Werner, A. A. J.,, 43
Westwood, Sidney, 2
White, ganger, viii, 38
Wickwar, Francis, 50
Woods, bar landlord, 21, 25, 27, 33, 46, 71, 81

www.ingramcontent.com/pod-product-compliance
Lightning Source LLC
LaVergne TN
LVHW091109080426
835509LV00007B/950